HIRING SECRETS FOR DIGITAL MARKETING AGENCIES

3 Key Roles To Help You Scale To A Million Dollars & Beyond

AZHAR SIDDIQUI

Copyright © 2023 by AZHAR SIDDIQUI.

All rights reserved.

No part of this publication may be reproduced, distributed, or transmitted in any form or by any means, including photocopying, recording, or other electronic or mechanical methods, without the prior written permission of the publisher, except in the case of brief quotations embodied in critical reviews and certain other noncommercial uses permitted by copyright law.

No fluff, no BS, just actionable steps to build a 7-figure marketing agency.

I've been fortunate enough to be able to watch Azhar drive the growth of his agency and establish their leadership in their market.

Read his book!!

– **SHAUN CLARK**
Co-founder at HighLevel

The "Hiring Secrets For Digital Marketing Agencies (3 Key Roles To Help You Scale To A Million Dollars & Beyond)" is the only book focused on hiring for digital marketing agencies out there.

In this book, Azhar details the unique methodology that helped 100s of digital marketing agency owners acquire & retain more clients and grow their agencies to multiple 7 figures. His methods aren't theory - they're actually proven inside his agency and hundreds of agencies that deploy RepStack VAs.

I've known Azhar for years, he's generous with his knowledge & a whip-smart operator. I have seen him build his Million-dollar agency by following the same hiring processes and making the right use of these roles.

The detailed steps and accessible breakdowns in this book are refreshing and invaluable. Follow his advice, put in the work & you'll hit your goals.

Now, when agency owners come to me for help with building up processes in their agency by hiring Marketing Associates, I'll gladly slide this book their way

– **JOSH NELSON**
Founder & CEO at Seven Figure Agency

 I have been a part of RepStack almost from inception. First as the coach of a membership group and now as the private coach to RepStack's Leadership Team. In all of my years of coaching, I have never worked with a team that so effectively embraces change. Every week, as I attend the leader's meeting, the report of actions completed sometimes feels endless. This team has a mission and is committed to making it happen.

The Siddiqui brothers are an up-and-coming powerhouse in the area of Digital Agency transformation. Most agencies do a fantastic job of taking care of their customers. However, they rarely establish an internal team specializing in their own agency growth. Once just one of these 3 key positions are filled, the agency owner will see incredible growth. As they hire all three positions, they will see exponential growth!

Azhar teaches from his direct example of how to build a digital marketing agency, step-by-step. I've seen few -- among many-- that have the credibility, experience, and heart to truly help people build a successful agency.

– JEFF FISHER
Chief Agency Growth Specialist at Jeff Fisher and Associate

Azhar teaches us from his own example the true power of leadership.

I've seen Azhar struggle to overcome the bottlenecks inside his own 14-year digital marketing journey and use his wisdom and learning experience to grow RepStack to multiple 7 figures within a couple of years.

Hiring the right talent takes the burden off your shoulders, instead of creating more problems for you to solve.

The most successful agency owners I know are not the smartest or hardest-working people but build up great teams that can execute their vision. I like how he explains the key roles to hire for and the best order of hiring them. The book "Hiring Secrets For Digital Marketing Agencies (3 Key Roles To Help You Scale To A Million Dollars & Beyond)" is a great resource for agency owners, as Azhar has worked with several 100 digital marketing agencies helping them build out successful and empowered teams.

– **Dennis Yu**
Chief Executive Officer at BlitzMetrics

 This book is perfect for people who are stuck in the initial stage of their marketing agency and want to grow.

I've seen many agency owners still trapped in the Freelancer trap. They have clients and are good at providing their services, but they struggle when it comes to matters like Marketing, Sales & Retention for their own Agency.

They forget that you need a team to achieve true financial freedom. A team ready to execute for you based on the systems that you already have in place. This is exactly where RepStack comes in.

This book does an amazing job of teaching you how to grow your agency and how to build the processes you need to take that agency to the next level, out of the freelancer trap, without you doing everything yourself.

– **ALEX SCHLINSKY**
Founder of Prospecting on Demand

If you're looking for a guide on how to hire talent for your Marketing Agency, then this book is for you.

It's the perfect guide for anyone who is looking to expand their business and needs help in finding and hiring marketing, sales, and account managers.

It contains detailed steps and explanations on how to go about the entire process, from start to finish.

You will learn everything there is to know about finding, vetting, and hiring a digital marketing agency that's the perfect fit for your business

I have several members hired who are part of the internal team at PipelinePRO. They have been indispensable assets to the team.

I have personally known Azhar and the Siddiqui brother for over 2 years. He has years of experience in this field, and he shares all of his knowledge in this book. You won't want to miss out on this!

– **ANDREW J. CASS**
Co-founder & CEO at Pipeline PRO

Azhar nails it with this one. This book is remarkably actionable - I challenge you to read it and implement the frameworks he lays out in detail. The way he explains "The Account Manager advantage and how hiring a team of account managers focuses on Client Success" is invaluable information.

– **JASON LOCKHART**
Founder of Kitchen and Bath Marketing Solutions

The "Hiring Secrets For Digital Marketing Agencies (3 Key Roles To Help You Scale To A Million Dollars & Beyond)" is the only book focused on hiring for digital marketing agencies out there.

In this book, Azhar details the unique methodology that helped 100s of digital marketing agency owners acquire & retain more clients and grow their agencies to multiple 7 figures.

Follow his Advice. Soak up everything he has to say!

– **LYN ASKIN**
CEO & Founder at Raxxar Digital Marketing

Table of Contents

Preface 14

Introduction 18

Chapter 1: The STUCK Agency Owner 23

    Not Enough Move Forward Conversations 25

    My 13-Year Grind As A Digital Marketing Agency Owner........27

    A Breakthrough 32

    The Key To Success Is Working With Virtual Associates............37

Chapter 2: The FREE Agency Owner..................................43

    Take A Look Behind The Scenes 44

    Discover Who And What An Associate Is......................47

    Virtual Assistant...49

    A Local Hire...50

    How John Victoria of Poliana Reached $1 Million in Annual Revenue in Just 5 Years..52

    How a Sales Development Rep Closed 92 Deals 56

    Account Manager Case Study: Asmaa............................59

    Becoming The Free Agency Owner................................61

Chapter 3: The Answer, Hire For 3 Key Roles....................64

    Your Agency Journey..71

    Marketing Associate..74

    Sales Development Representative................................80

Account Manager 84

Chapter 4: Secret #1: The First Brick in The Foundation, The Marketing Associate 87

    Getting Back To The Basics 92

    The Marketing Associate Is The Anchor 96

    A Breakdown of the Marketing Associate Role 100

    Benchmarks You Should Expect 102

    Case Study of a Marketing Associate 108

Chapter 5: Hiring, Onboarding, and Training your Marketing Associate 113

    Job Descriptions 114

    Example One 114

    Example Two 117

    Skills You Should Look Out For 118

    Skills Explained 120

    The Interview Process 121

    Communication Is Key 124

    Hiring Process Checklist 127

    Onboarding Your New Marketing Associate 129

    Management, Accountability, and Ongoing Training 131

    90 Day RepStack Success Academy Learning Path 133

Chapter 6: The Marketing Associate Case Studies 136

    Owner of Floor Coating Marketers, and Remsha, Digital Marketing Associate 137

Owner of AE Design Co., and Hamza, Digital Marketing Associate 142

Owner of Type B Studio and Salman, Digital Marketing Associate 147

Owners of Beyond Creative Digital Growth Agency, and Hajra, Digital Marketing Specialist 150

Chapter 7: Secret 2: The Sales Development Rep 155

Position Overview 157

Sample 1 161

Sample 2 162

The Benefits of Working with a Sales Development Rep 164

Having The Mechanics In Place 169

Chapter 8: Hiring, Onboarding, and Training your Sales Development Rep (SDR) 172

Step One: Attracting The Right Sales Development Rep 173

Step Two: Sales Development Rep Job Description 175

Sales Development Rep Job Description Samples 178

Step Three: Interviewing Sales Development Reps 183

Step Four: Onboarding and Training Your Sales Development Rep 187

Onboarding Checklist 189

Chapter 9: Successful SDR Case Studies 192

How a Kitchen Remodeling SEO Owner Landed More Clients With A SDR..193

How Service Legend Was Able To Increase Sales With Their Sales Executive 198

SDR 2.0s: The Future of Sales Development Reps 202

Chapter 10: Secret 3 Unlocked: The Account Manager 204

    What An Account Manager Can Do For You 206

    Overcommunication Using Account Managers is Great for Business 209

    The Right Time To Hire An Account Manager 211

Chapter 11: Hiring, Onboarding, and Training Your Account Manager 218

    Hiring An Account Manager 219

    Interview For An Account Manager 228

    Onboarding Your New Account Manager 230

    90 Day RepStack Success Academy Training Plan 231

    Ongoing Training, Management, & Accountability 234

    Account Manager End-Of-Day Reports Example: 236

Chapter 12: The Account Manager Case Studies 238

    CEO Tree Service Digital had an Incredible Experience Working with an Account Manager 240

    Owner of TopLine Growth made Tremendous Progress Working with an Account Manager 244

    Owner of Raxxar Digital Marketing Agency & His Account Manager Experience 248

Conclusion 253

Bonus Chapter! 263

Preface

The day was January 5, 2019. I was at the mall with my wife on a beautiful Saturday morning. Suddenly my phone rang, the call was from one of my clients who was upset about a spelling error on his website.

My clients were my top priority, I knew I would do anything to make sure they were happy. So, I jumped on the call trying to see what I could do. My wife noticed how I could not even spare a day for her despite it being the weekend.

The call went on for over half an hour, and by the time it ended, I could not focus on my family time. My wife gave me a cold stare and the weekend descended into a deepfreeze. This has been my life for 11 years now – no weekends, no vacations, no financial stability, and constantly running after clients.

I was stuck in a vicious circle as a digital marketing agency owner.

4 years later I am running an agency evaluated at $25 million with multiple 7 figures in annual revenue and 200+ people.

So, what made the difference in my second agency?

In my first agency, I was wearing all the hats.

I felt like I couldn't win. When we had a good month in sales, no one was working on marketing, when marketing activities got going, current clients got neglected and so on and on and on.

A good month at Marketing was a bad month for Sales. And a good month of Sales meant chaos at operations/ client success.

By managing my agency's Marketing, Sales, and operations as well as being its CEO I had a lot on my plate.

Whenever I won at one thing, other things brought me down.

- I didn't have a roadmap for success
- I didn't know my way out

But apart from that, I didn't know I was stuck in a vicious cycle

I didn't have much choice, so I kept doing what I was doing.

The only difference was that this time

- I had a coach to guide me
- I had a roadmap for success.

Fortunately, my strategy worked. The first time around I was being the jack of all trades but this time I had specialists to do all those things for me.

Discovering the Secret...

What I'm going to share with you is the strategy that helped me scale my agency to 200+ people within 24 months

Now, this isn't some get-rich-quick scheme, I am not going to BS you.

It's the secret that we have fine-tuned in our business and applied for our clients over & over again. It can do the same for you.

I can't promise that the road will be easy, there will be some difficult decisions and some hard work.

But this Strategy has transformed my life and the lives of many others we've worked with.

Throughout this book, I will share my Hiring Secrets that helped me scale to 7 figures and beyond and show you how you can experience more success, Freedom, and Impact.

Who is Azhar Siddiqui & Why You should read this Book?

My name is Azhar Siddiqui, I am going to teach you how to hire the right talent, set up processes, and Retain clients to deliver amazing & systemized results. This Book "Hiring Secrets For Digital Marketing Agencies" reveals the key strategies that drive a Million-dollar agency.

There are plenty of agencies out there surviving at $10k a month. They don't have processes, enough leads, clients, and most importantly right human resources. My aim is to help them scale so they too can get out of the Rat race.

My Job is to help you scale your agency and give you three things

- ➢ More Money
- ➢ More Freedom
- ➢ More Impact

I don't know where you are in your Agency journey. But I promise that after reading this book you'll be on the right path and be able to scale to 7 figures.

Introduction

This book, **Hiring Secrets for Digital Marketing Agencies** is a guide for agency owners who want to scale to a million dollars and beyond.

Through this book, you'll learn how to:

- Strategically place & hire for internal roles inside your agency
- Scale to 7 figures and beyond by placing people inside 3 key roles
- My complete 8-step hiring process and how you can save well over 7 figures by outsourcing talent

This book will reveal top hiring secrets to unlock massive growth inside your marketing agency. Now I know that sounds like a bold statement, but think about it. If you focus on hiring for strategic roles that work inside your agency, you can unlock more time, freedom, and money.

I am going to share real-life examples of other digital marketing agencies that have gone to seven figures and beyond by just focusing on the 3-role framework.

Struggling with your agency?

Well so was I, I found myself stuck doing the day-to-day of my agency but then I realized the 3 key roles that were crucial to activating massive growth.

There are three reasons digital marketing agencies fail. And, when I share more of my story with you in a moment, you'll see that I've faced all of them myself.

1. Owners don't have enough time to focus on their agency's marketing
2. I have a ton of leads but lack a proper sales team and process
3. I don't have enough time to communicate with all my clients

You may be at a point where you as an agency owner are struggling, and so was I but today I can proudly say that I'm able to influence and bring leads anytime I interact within a community.

Discovering the Road Map

- This book is a guide to unlocking the hiring secrets that will allow your marketing agency to scale to 7 figures and beyond
- The book provides a process for reaching this goal in 24-36 months, with real-life examples of agency owners who were once stuck in a vicious circle of doing marketing, sales, and account management themselves.
- The key to success is delegating tasks to three key members: a marketing associate, a sales development representative, and an account manager.

I was the bottleneck inside my agency...

Today I run a 7-figure marketing agency and a multiple 7 figure VA placement agency. We've got a team of 200+ full-time employees and were recently featured in Entrepreneur.com. But I will say that wasn't always my experience.

My first marketing agency, Agua was a generalist agency focusing on providing SEO, Paid Ads, and Website Development but I had the wrong model. I was selling a website for a one-time fee; it was all project-based work and I had 0 monthly retainers.

- I was stuck in the vicious cycle of doing everything from Sales to Marketing and Account Management
- Experiencing burnout and exhaustion

The Turning Point.

However, after I discovered the right model and started getting monthly retainer clients, my business started to pick up. I went from a generalist agency to niching down and focusing on hiring the right people, in the right roles inside my agency. Most importantly, I found belief that all it took was having 3 specific roles hired internally.

- The Marketing Associate
- The Sales Development Rep
- The Account Manager

Hiring the right people is one of the most important things you can do when starting a digital marketing agency. I've worked with at least 250+ digital marketing agency owners, and I've seen firsthand how the right team can make all the difference. When you have a team of talented, dedicated individuals working towards a common goal, there's no limit to what you can achieve. But finding the right people can be a challenge. With so many options out there, it can be tough to know where to start. Here are a few tips that I've found to be helpful when hiring talent for your agency.

First, take your time. Don't rush into hiring just anyone. It's important to find someone who is a good fit for your company and who shares your vision for the future.

Second, don't be afraid to invest in talent. A top-notch team will be worth its weight in gold.

And finally, always be on the lookout for new talent. The digital marketing landscape is constantly changing, and you need to make sure you have the best possible team in order to stay ahead of the curve.

I'm excited to unpack this model in detail for you as we go through this book because I know the massive impact it can have. There are countless case studies of guys like

- John Victoria, who reached $1 Million in Annual Revenue by focusing on getting his marketing right and hiring a talented Marketing Specialist
- Josh Nelson, who used his SDR to close over **92** deals in under 3 months
- Lyn Askin, who enabled his Account Manager to take charge of over 20 SEO clients, including project management and all client communications

You can put stock in what I'm going to be sharing with you because I have done it and am currently doing it, and I've helped others do the same.

I applaud you for taking the time to think about your plan, invest in yourself, and figure out what it is you need to do to get things going.

Chapter 1:

The STUCK Agency Owner

This is your guide to reaching that $1 million mark for your digital marketing agency in the next 24 to 36 months.

Though that might look like a bold statement, especially if you've been in this industry for years, it's in no way impossible. You might think that's out of your reach if:

- You've been grinding at the wheel year after year to make the money you've been dreaming of.

- More than likely, you've traded your 9-5 job for one that you've now realized is a 24/7 operation.

- You may have come to the point that you just don't know how to move over some of the biggest challenges in the industry.

- You are stuck in a vicious circle, doing your agency's marketing, sales, and account management.

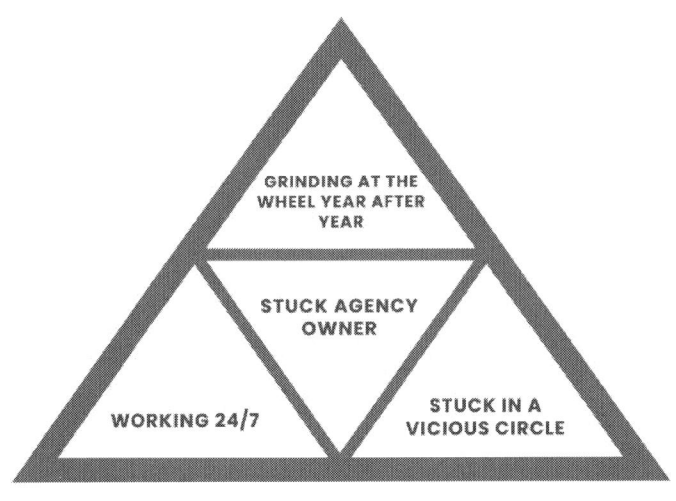

> *If you can't imagine yourself making $1 million in the next three years, you could call yourself a stuck agency owner*

This book is going to guide you through the easy-to-follow process that will show you exactly how to reach that number in the next 2 to 3 years.

The traditional way of growing a digital marketing agency has you doing a lot of work every single day. You're constantly sending out cold outreach emails and messages that may have you rethinking your life decisions. There is nothing more discouraging than not receiving any replies from all of your cold messages, and the ones that you do get a reply from say, "unsubscribe me."

Not Enough Move Forward Conversations

This leads to you not booking enough discovery calls or strategy sessions. You know that the real magic happens when you're able to get a prospective client on that call. But it's hard to focus when you're being pulled in so many directions.

There is no doubt that you're putting in the work. I've been in this industry for decades, and I know what it takes to become successful. For years, I was a one-man crew running on fumes just to make $150k a year. To some, that might seem like a nice yearly wage to make six figures. But not being able to take my agency over the $300,000 /year no matter how hard I worked for seven years in a row had me second-guessing everything.

Unlike when I started out (of course, without a team), you may already have a team you're probably consistently messaging and managing. Perhaps, you might be dealing with freelancers who don't seem to cut it. Or maybe, finding reputable talent is one of your main stress points because you have to rely on others to do some of the heavy lifting.

You're in this business for a reason. It's your passion. You love what you do. But you want to take it all to the next level and not be constantly stressed out about what has become 'work'.

At this point in managing your digital marketing agency, you've started running on fumes. You're doing everything you know to do in order to be successful. But managing it all on your own has become a hassle. It's rewarding to be a boss of a successful company, but you can only go so far on your own.

There is no reason to be a stuck agency owner. Instead, your marketing agency should be running on autopilot. You should be moving away from a one-man bank, making only 100k a year, to the path of turning your agency into a million-dollar+ growing business.

What if you could focus on growing your agency instead of just keeping it afloat?

What if you could move away from the busy day-to-day 'work' and let it run on its own?

"

What if you could move away from the busy day-to-day 'work' and let it run on its own? Can you see yourself taking a step back and watching your marketing agency take off while you remain relaxed and in control?

You've been at the forefront of your agency for so long that it must be hard to imagine things growing steadily without you taking care of sales and client relations yourself. But there comes a time when you need to step back and focus on marketing your own agency instead of creating all the ads for your clients. There is most definitely a way, and I intend to share the map with you.

My 13-Year Grind As A Digital Marketing Agency Owner

While attending Minnesota State University way back in 2002, I learned the importance of websites and marketing for small businesses. However, getting my first digital marketing client took me another six years.

An introvert by nature, I had no clue how to sell. I knew that in order to build a business, I needed to be able to sell. This led me to take a job at Future Shop, a sister company of Best Buy in Canada.

Their model was different. I was hired as a product expert, and I got paid on commissions. Around the same time, I also married and had a family to take care of now. I had to get out of my shell and become a sales pro if I wanted to make a decent living.

Luckily, I know that if I have a roadmap and put in a little extra effort than my peers, I can be the underdog no one saw coming.

Within six months, I was crushing it at sales, selling complete camera packages with memory cards, cases, and the coveted extended warranties.

As I grew through the ranks at Best Buy, becoming a Department Manager and leading Canada's top computer sales team, I continued to dream about starting my agency. On my bus rides back and forth to work, I would read magazines like Inc and Fortune to keep the dream alive.

I received my first break when I spoke to Justin, a salesperson, and a good old-fashioned Alberta-born computer geek, about my agency idea. The same day he was in! We had a company name registered the same week and closed our first $350 website deals the first month in business. I'm proud of the fact that my agency still services those first few clients we got.

Having a partner as excited as me was a game-changer for me. I would focus on sales while Justin spoke with contractors overseas to get the work done.

Over the next two years, we grew the agency to about $100,000 a year at which point Justin parted ways to pursue his career in retail. I bought him out for $10k.

My friend Adam was finishing his degree in entrepreneurship and showed interest, so I gave him Justin's share and brought him on as the next partner. I brought Adam on as a partner in 2011, and we ran the agency together till 2018. Adam and I were able to earn around $300,000 a year.

When I went full-time with my agency in 2011, I thought, "Now this business will just explode." Little did I know that a time of ultimate grind was just starting.

"

Little did I know that a time of ultimate grind was just starting

"

Looking back on those years, I can clearly see all the issues we should have tackled. But you know what they say: hindsight is 20/20.

Here are just some of the things we didn't do correctly:

- Both partners had no distinctions in their job roles. We were both working on the same things at the same time. This created friction.

- Taking too much time to make decisions. We were just scared of losing the money, which was tight.

- Not having a niche to focus on. We were a generalist agency and closed anything we could get our hands on.

- No set process for our own marketing. When business was down, we would jump on calls, call old clients and do whatever it took to get some sales in.

- Once we closed a few deals, we would get busy completing the work for clients and catering to their every wish while losing focus on sales and marketing.

- **NO DISTINCTIONS IN THE JOB ROLES**
- **TAKING TOO MUCH TIME TO MAKE DECISIONS**
- **NOT HAVING A NICHE TO FOCUS ON**
- **NO SET PROCESS FOR OUR OWN MARKETING**

Those were some tough years. We took home $60k each in a good year and $35k in a bad year.

In 2017, Adam finally got himself a high-paying job and stepped back from the day-to-day of the agency. He gave me a number so I could buy him out. That year, I made a lot of decisions and fast. I made more sales than both of us combined. At the end of 2017, I was able to buy out Adam.

This time I decided to go for it alone. I could take home $100k easily. However, I was still stuck in that vicious circle. I'd go from completing some marketing activity to moving right into sales to doing account management and back to marketing.

A Breakthrough

Then a breakthrough came when I signed up for Josh Nelson's Seven Figure Agency coaching program. I had read his book earlier, and everything he talked about really clicked with me.

Investing in a world-class coaching program was the best decision I ever made. I quickly identified 2 to 3 clients to whom I was delivering amazing results and identified niches where I could grow really fast.

I was a part of a group of peers who were doing exactly the same and growing their agencies real fast.

I finally stuck to launching RepStack with my brothers, focusing on digital marketing agencies and providing virtual associates (so much more than just the typical virtual assistant) in 3 key roles. From there, things started moving at a breakneck speed for me.

Today as I write this book, I am leading a team of 180 people that is growing by 30 a month. We service 100+ digital marketing agencies, helping them break the same vicious circle I was stuck in for years.

If I have done my job correctly, this book should help you identify why we get stuck as agency owners and what we should be doing to get back on track and take our agencies to $1 million a year and beyond. I've Been Where You Stand Now

I completely understand the struggles you are experiencing with your marketing agency. I struggled to fulfill all of the different roles in the business. Though I rocked at being able to outsource work for different content, social media, SEO, and web development, I struggled to be the sales manager, marketing associate, and account manager. These are often the last roles any digital marketing agency owner hires for.

When you are doing everything in your business yourself, even if you outsource different parts of your agency, you're going to get burned out.

Your agency won't be able to grow when you are being pulled in too many directions.

Believe it or not, I learned how to be a good salesman by working for Best Buy. I did that for seven years as I developed my own techniques for bringing in big sales. It was my hero's journey as I moved away from a life of being an introvert and learned how to really connect with people.

That's what I loved about owning a digital marketing agency. I was making connections with people from around the world and providing them with marketing solutions that skyrocketed their businesses. But my own agency struggled to have the same type of launch. I was so focused on fulfilling the needs of others that I struggled to accomplish the same level of growth.

I used to dream about having an agency that helped other people. I would imagine having over one hundred employees in a successful work environment. And now that dream is a reality. Launching RepStack to help other digital marketing agencies is a dream come true. With over 180 team members and counting, I'm seeing bigger growth than ever before.

This is all a part of my journey. The same type of journey I want to take you through to achieve this same level of success. While most agency owners struggle to be their own sales manager, marketing director, and account manager, I'm going to show you how to, instead, grow this part of your agency to make all of your dreams come true as well.

Can you imagine having a long list (of more than 1500 names) of prospective clients? How about a successful CRM system that any sales employee would be able to navigate?

Growth happens when you are able to automate parts of your agency. I understand what it's like not to have time to grow or to become too busy with the day-to-day agenda of the agency. But I also found a way to become a huge success by learning what parts of the agency could be managed on autopilot.

As digital marketing agency owners, we need to eat our own dog food

,,

I've owned my own digital marketing agency in Canada for the last thirteen years. In the beginning, I was my own marketing person – my own salesperson. I was the only account manager. And I also know a lot of people who do that in their companies.

Digital marketing agencies are experts when it comes to marketing for their clients, but they neglect their own marketing. They are so busy with the daily operations of their agencies that they find it difficult to grow their own agency.

Does this sound familiar to you?

Are these the biggest struggles you are facing as well?

When was the last time your agency saw a sudden increase in growth?

My company, RepStack, helps other digital marketing agency experts have exponential growth. I understand the struggles of being an agency owner, but I also know how to solve many of the problems that owners face each day.

The Key To Success Is Working With Virtual Associates

There is a process to gaining success. When I work with agency owners, they often want to jump right in by working with a sales assistant. But if you don't have certain systems in place that are automating your business, then a sales assistant isn't going to do much for you.

Instead, you're going to learn what a sales assistant, marketing assistant, and account manager can do for you. Most importantly, you'll learn in what order each of these individuals should be hired. You'll get real examples of how to find these full-time individuals, and even get to use ads from this book that you'll be able to post online to get the best possible candidate. It's a step-by-step process that you'll be able to follow easily, so that by the time you finish this book, you'll already be seeing growth in your agency.

"

I can say with a high degree of confidence that learning to step back and delegate the three different roles this book focuses on is what leads to significant growth in your business

"

I can say with a high degree of confidence that learning to step back and delegate the three different roles this book focuses on is what will lead to significant growth in your business. I've done it many times. I've tested it many times. And now, I help other agencies do the same thing. My team is great at what it does because of the methods I developed. There is a particular order that you'll be able to pick up in no time to start implementing today.

How do you know if you're ready for a virtual associate? Take a look at the following questions. If you can answer yes to at least three of them, then you know you're ready:

- Are you making at least $10,000 a month in agency revenue?
- Do you have at least two full-time employees (including yourself)?
- Do you want to hire a full-time employee without thinking about long-term contracts, W-2, etc.?
- Are you interested in hiring a paid advertising specialist, i.e., social media marketing?
- Are you looking for an agency sales development representative who can close 5 figure deals just like you?
- Are you handling all inbound and outbound calls and need to free up your time?
- Do you want to focus on the strategic aspect of your business while letting your associate handle all client-facing activities?

DO YOU KNOW

- ARE YOU MAKING AT LEAST $10,000 A MONTH IN AGENCY REVENUE?
- DO YOU HAVE AT LEAST TWO FULL-TIME EMPLOYEES (INCLUDING YOURSELF)?
- DO YOU WANT TO HIRE A FULL-TIME EMPLOYEE WITHOUT THINKING ABOUT LONG-TERM CONTRACTS, W-2, ETC?
- ARE YOU INTERESTED IN HIRING A PAID ADVERTISING SPECIALIST I.E. SOCIAL MEDIA MARKETING?
- ARE YOU LOOKING FOR AN AGENCY SALES DEVELOPMENT REPRESENTATIVE WHO CAN CLOSE 5 FIGURE DEALS JUST LIKE YOU?
- ARE YOU HANDLING ALL INBOUND AND OUTBOUND CALLS AND NEED TO FREE UP YOUR TIME?
- DO YOU WANT TO FOCUS ON THE STRATEGIC ASPECT OF YOUR BUSINESS WHILE LETTING YOUR ASSOCIATE HANDLE ALL CLIENT-FACING ACTIVITIES?

Working with an associate helps free up your time from the daily operations of your agency. They can perform your core activities, giving you more time to focus on growing your agency.

Rather than wasting time and resources doing it all yourself, you can invest in thinking strategically to activate massive growth.

An associate helps to reduce agency costs by lowering overhead and operating costs. In turn, they help you scale your business operations quickly.

One of the biggest benefits of working with an associate is they offer 24/7 customer service by working in international time zones.

While all digital marketing agency owners like to be in control and do everything themselves, eventually, you're going to run out of energy if you follow this pattern. It's not possible to be the jack of all trades. With associates, you can compensate for your agency's skill gap. Associates also provide you with a pipeline of extra skill sets. Being a digital marketing agency veteran, I know how exhausting it is to do it all yourself. You're trying to make the sales calls while also planning local events to attend. As soon as you close the deals, you have to move into account manager mode. Then when those projects finish, you're back into the marketing manager's shoes. It's a vicious cycle that will drain all the energy right out of you.

"

It's a vicious cycle that will drain all the energy right out of you.

"

Outsourcing this work to full-time individuals is the key to success. Most agency owners do this last, willing to outsource only specific work, such as web development and SEO, to part-timers. But it should be the other way around and done in a particular order. That way, YOU, the agency owner, can focus on growth! In this book, you're going to learn how to use full-time, dedicated associates to grow your agency. While you might have been able to outsource other agency work to part-timers on Fiverr and Upwork, these individuals are not long-term dedicated. Plus, it's very hard to hire from these platforms because it's time-consuming and dull.

- Instead, you'll be given the necessary resources to grow your agency. You'll learn: The right time to hire each of the three types of associates, and why there is a particular order.
- You'll learn where to find dedicated associates and be given examples of hiring ads you can use right away.

- You'll discover the wide range of capabilities of the three types of associates and what they can do for your agency.

- Most importantly, you'll start to see your agency operating on autopilot.

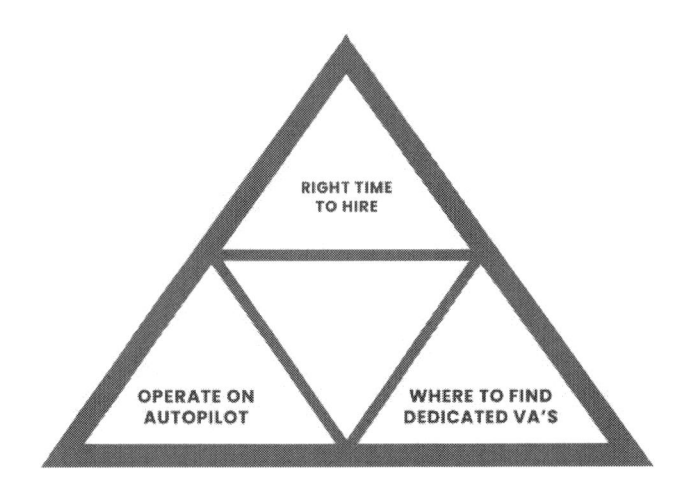

```
         RIGHT TIME
          TO HIRE

OPERATE ON          WHERE TO FIND
 AUTOPILOT          DEDICATED VA'S
```

Until you start to trust people, you won't be able to head down the path of having a $1 million growth track. This book will help you put people into the roles you are used to. In the long run, your agency saves a lot of money, and you save precious time.

By the end of this book, you'll have all the tools you need to successfully hire the right associates that will grow your business. You'll get to review real case studies and see how associates have helped other digital marketing agencies.

Everything I did to become a huge success; you're going to be able to do them as well. You'll be able to focus on marketing your own agency instead of solving all your clients' problems. You'll move from being overworked and stressed to having more free time on your hands to enjoy leisure time. This book is based on real-life experience. I've had the $1 million success, but I don't share that with you to brag. Instead, I want to impress upon you that what I'm going to be sharing here isn't from a book that I read.

It's not just some theory that I think might be a good way to grow a digital marketing agency.

I've done it, and I've lived it. I've shared it with others who went through the same struggles, and I've seen them succeed.

And now, I'm excited to share it with you so you can achieve your greatest dreams as well.

Chapter 2:

The FREE Agency Owner

Ever wonder how other marketing agency owners are having the time of their lives traveling and on a beach? All the while, you're rethinking your life decisions. You're acting as unpaid marketing, sales, and account manager and can't even find the time to think of a vacation.

Why is it that you can't find the time to grow your agency while other agency owners have their entire business on autopilot?

Or that you are struggling to connect with your prospective clients?

Why is it that you have to hustle so hard just to close the last deal before the end of the month so you can pay your bills?

Or that you have a hard time retaining the clients that you do have?

Why is it that you can't make the type of money as other agency owners when you feel you're doing the same work and putting in even more time than them?

The successful agency owners that you've witnessed, those that are spending more time with family and doing the things they love, are what I call the free agency owners. They are no longer stuck because they understand how to make their agency work for them.

A free agency owner is someone who isn't wearing multiple hats anymore and has mastered the art of delegation. They trust their teams and have hired professionals for certain roles at precisely the right time.

Now, the free agency owner is traveling, enjoying the freedom that having money and time provides. They are not stuck in a 24/7 'job' that is stressful, frustrating, and demanding. Instead, they are free to do as they please while still being in full control of their marketing agency.

Take A Look Behind The Scenes

So, what is actually happening? How did the stuck agency owner go from being stressed out and overworked to being completely free?

The free agency owner is still landing five-figure clients. The free agency owner is clearly making money but also saving money. And they are able to focus on growing their agency instead of catering to clients all day or working long hours to complete the projects for clients.

Here's what is happening behind the scenes. The free agency owner has strategically placed managers and associates into three key roles: marketing associate, sales development representative, and account manager.

THREE KEY ROLES

Marketing Associate · Sales Associate Rep · Account Manager

Your first thought is that you need to hurry up and hire these three key roles. Or you might be uncertain about hiring three more employees when you're struggling to make a salary yourself.

But it's not as straightforward as placing an ad online for those three key roles. There is a right time to establish these three different positions, and if you don't establish them in the right order, your agency won't run on autopilot.

The truth is that you save a lot of money when you can fill these key roles. Whether you hire locally or from outside your state or country, I guarantee you will save time and money from the get-go. Imagine your take home is $150k after paying all contractors. And, in most cases, you are paying yourself $150k for doing sales and account management. You claim that you are amazing at account management, but I can assure you that you are not even doing a great job in sales, not to mention account management.

Now visualize hiring a marketing assistant ($8-$15/ hour outside of the USA and $15 to $25 inside the USA). If you hired this person overseas, take $23,000 from your take-home and spend it on this key role. You just saved $127,000 by not doing this job yourself and simultaneously ensuring that your agency's marketing engine will continue to work without you.

Now do the same by hiring a Sales assistant and an account manager.

Unless you change your mind set about these key roles and get the right people placed there, you will continue to take home the money you are currently earning but with no growth in sight. That's usually the case; trust me, I tried it for 13 years.

Getting the right people in the right position is how you put your marketing agency into sudden growth mode. Every agency owner needs to take a step back and grow their agency using these key roles. Putting your trust in a skilled manager or associate lets you focus on the most important aspect of your role in your agency: GROWTH. That's how you reach the $1 million mark.

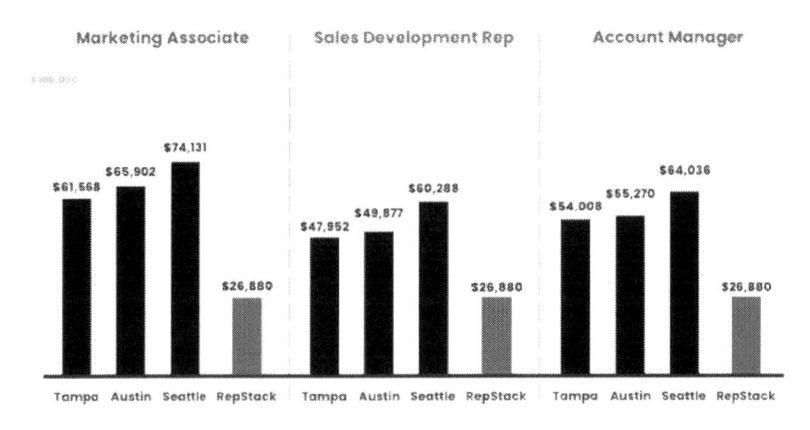

	Marketing Associate				Sales Development Rep				Account Manager			
	Tampa	Austin	Seattle	RepStack	Tampa	Austin	Seattle	RepStack	Tampa	Austin	Seattle	RepStack
	$61,568	$65,902	$74,131	$26,880	$47,952	$49,877	$60,288	$26,880	$54,008	$55,270	$64,036	$26,880

Discover Who And What An Associate Is

You've experienced outsourcing work before in your marketing agency. You have gone through the hassle of finding a decent copywriter or someone who can build websites. Having scoured through different online freelance websites such as Fiverr or Up Work, you understand how difficult it can be to find a social media manager or SEO specialist.

> *The idea of hiring virtual associates, at first, doesn't always settle well in your mind.*

At first, the idea of hiring virtual associates doesn't always settle well in your mind. But before you can start thinking about how to hire a virtual associate, you have to discover who they are and what they are capable of doing.

The three key roles that these associates fill are the marketing, sales, and accounts positions. Normally these three roles are filled last in a marketing agency when it should be the other way around to spark growth mode.

These are the three jobs that agency owners usually struggle with every day. It becomes a vicious cycle, jumping from one role to the next instead of delegating this work. By establishing particular mechanics with these three roles, your agency will begin to run on autopilot.

1. The **marketing associate** is the person who is going to handle outreach programs and set up key marketing activities to capture prospective clients. They are the ones that are creating the long list of prospective clients who are interested, running email outreach campaigns, managing social media, etc. This person will eventually lead an established marketing department.

2. The **sales development representative** is the one who has practical experience in booking appointments. They proactively reach out to clients your marketing associate has been targeting via emails, opt-in funnels, etc., and then book appointments for you or the sales manager. This extrovert has no problem talking to clients and creating those long-lasting relationships.

3. The **account manager's** biggest responsibility is retention. The clients you have worked so hard to close need to stay with your agency for years to come. The right person in this role will manage your clients like a pro giving them individual attention, resolving issues before they happen, and upselling when possible. Your biggest advantage is that you now have a buffer between you and the clients. You know now that a client won't be calling you at dinner, causing you to drop everything you are doing and frantically fix the spelling mistake on the about us page.

Those are the three key roles that create growth for any digital marketing agency when hired in a particular order. Though you're starting to gain an understanding of what these three key roles can do for your agency, you also have to know who these associates are.

It's important to understand the options you have when going out to hire for these key roles — Virtual Assistants, Virtual Associates (our specialty), and hiring locally.

Virtual Assistant

Most agency owners, including me, start here. An associate can be found on platforms like Fiverr and Up Work and are usually the most affordable option. They usually work project to project, but you can also find them to work full-time for you.

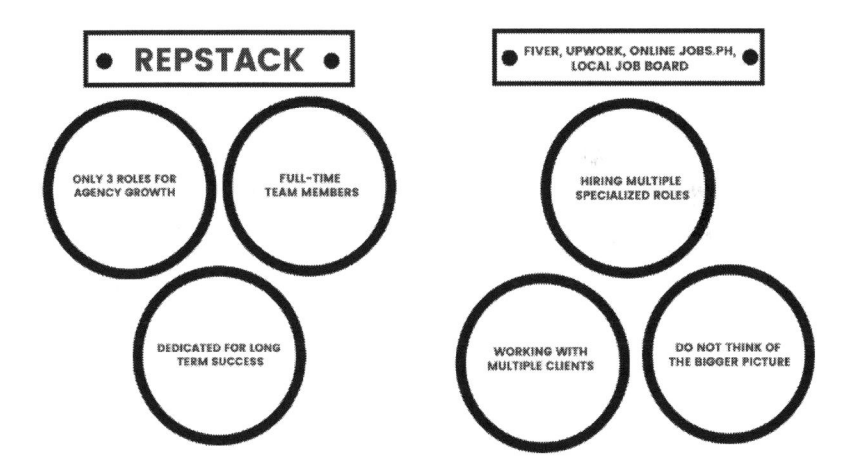

REPSTACK
- ONLY 3 ROLES FOR AGENCY GROWTH
- FULL-TIME TEAM MEMBERS
- DEDICATED FOR LONG TERM SUCCESS

FIVER, UPWORK, ONLINE JOBS.PH, LOCAL JOB BOARD
- HIRING MULTIPLE SPECIALIZED ROLES
- WORKING WITH MULTIPLE CLIENTS
- DO NOT THINK OF THE BIGGER PICTURE

The common issue with hiring a virtual associate on Fiverr and Upwork is that you must go through a grueling process to find the person, only to find out they are not what they said they were. They are also usually working on multiple projects at the same time, so it becomes hard for them to focus on your agency's vision.

A virtual associate is a long-term associate that is dedicated and hard-working. This is really an entry-level manager who can grow in the role they are placed in.

They are really your team members and will easily buy into your company's long-term vision. All you have to do is make available a level playing field, be willing to coach and train them, and see them soar.

They not only solve the initial problem but also think of other solutions as they become more familiar with their role. Though they, too, need initial training to be successful with your agency, they become a trustworthy associate you can let manage your agency while you take a step back.

A Local Hire

This is a very good option, too, and this person can do everything a virtual associate can do but at your office or be in the same city as you are. The downside here is that this person will cost more.

As I write this book, during the COVID-19 pandemic, most agency owners have moved their in-house teams to work from home too. I have seen multiple seven-figure agency owners hire outside of their home state and countries and get amazing results.

The pandemic has really changed our mindset about hiring locally. You now have access to the entire world to source the best talent for your agency.

However, hiring locally still remains a great option for many agency owners, and others now have hybrid teams. If you choose this path, you will have to find talent that fits within your agency's culture and budget. I recently had Shaun Clark on my podcast "Virtual Associate – the agency growth machine." Shaun is the co-founder of HighLevel; the biggest digital marketing agency focused on CRM in a market of 15000+ users as of January 2022.

When asked how he treats his local and overseas staff, he let me in on a secret. According to Shaun, his 200+ employees are based worldwide and are all treated equally. The big secret that no one realizes is that we have access to amazing talent from all around the world, so why not add team members from anywhere as long as they are the right fit? You can listen to the complete episode of the podcast by scanning the QR code below:

How John Victoria of Poliana Reached $1 Million in Annual Revenue in Just 5 Years

REPSTACK CASE STUDY

HOW JOHN VICTORIA OF POLIANA REACHED $1 MILLION IN ANNUAL REVENUE IN JUST 5 YEARS

JOHN VICTORIA | RIJA FATIMA

To give you a good idea of what a virtual associate is capable of, I'll introduce a case study for each of the three key roles you should incorporate into your agency to spark growth mode.

The first virtual associate you'll consider for your agency is a marketing assistant.

When I was recently talking to John Victoria, owner and founder of Poliana, he had a great story for me about his experience with Rija, his newest marketing assistant. Founded in 2016 and having over 70+ years of collective digital marketing experience, Poliana has brought together a superhero team of online marketers to change the game for home service providers. FYI, John recently hit the seven-figure mark after just 5 years in the business.

John started his business at the tender age of twenty. It was challenging initially because he had no prior business experience, but with time and a few good mentors, John managed to not only sustain his business but scale it to seven figures!

Growing up in a family where all the men were in the Navy, John followed in those footsteps by attending the Navy academy for officers. It was through this experience that John realized he wanted more in his life. He dove into the internet world to learn online sales and self-development through mastermind groups.

One of John's core values is always looking toward the next possibility. His wealth of knowledge at such a young age will benefit any digital marketing agency owner.

As I was talking to John, I asked him about his unique agency, Poliana, and what his team was doing differently for his niche and industry. He explained, "We believe driving meaningful business results to your business. We don't care much for vanity metrics like the number of likes on your Facebook page, how many views/impressions your ad got, or how many emails you received. We're focused on how we can get you qualified homeowners calling your business.

We believe in taking personal responsibility to identify new opportunities, solve potential issues, and create plans that will help us succeed in your campaign. We aren't sitting around waiting for things to happen…we're getting out there to get you ready for the future of our campaign and digital marketing."

With such a unique message and mission, I knew that John would also need a special marketing associate to help him fulfill his mission to his clients. So as the conversation turned toward Rija, his marketing associate, I was curious to know how she was getting along with his team after a year together.

He said, "From the interview to the first few weeks in the company, I've been really impressed with how Rija works, her attitude, and her proactiveness. She met the core values we are looking for in this agency.

"She's very result-oriented, accountable, has a high level of integrity, and a great team player. Most of my team are introverts, so it's great to have Rija around because she is more extroverted. She's not only reaching out but explaining to her team members the things she wants to coordinate.

"Rija even took on a leadership role for a small project we are doing internally."

After doing a post-interview with John Victoria, it was clear that Rija has been a phenomenal asset to the team. She has helped John and her co-workers set up all their marketing mechanisms. Currently, she is handling an outreach program for Poliana, helping with webinar registrations, and setting up other key marketing activities. It's clear to see why she is a virtual associate and not just a virtual assistant.

Her proactive and dedicated approach really suits the core values at Poliana. She really is one of the key players in the company.

❝

It's clear to see why she is a virtual associate and not just a virtual assistant.

❞

Rija is a great young professional who is newly married and plans on building a great career in digital marketing. Over the last year, as Poliana hit its $1 million revenue mark, Rija has been at the forefront of Polianas internal marketing, bringing in new deals with better margins using amazing marketing we tend to do for our clients anyways — only for ourselves this time!

When I had the chance to catch up with Rija, I learned from our conversation that she tackles several activities every day through her basecamp portal, where she can communicate with all of her Poliana team members.

She stated, "I like to stay connected with my team members to address any bottlenecks or other foreseen issues so they can be addressed and resolved quickly."

"After connecting with my team members, I'll address the list of assignments I've been given. My normal process is to complete those assignments marked urgent first, then move on to the less urgent assignments."

"Every day is a little different, but some of those tasks I've been assigned include writing a new cold call script in Google Docs."

"Other times, I'll be assisting a 4-week outreach campaign to gather 100 new prospects and also contacting each person on that new list. I'll then reach out to prospective clients through social media, using the Poliana pages. This helps Poliana grow as more clients discover the agency and understand what services they offer."

"In addition to contacting clients on social media, I'll also call prospective clients using HighLevel."

"If I've finished with my tasks for the day, I'll also spend time with continuing education to become the best marketing assistant."

"At the end of each working day, I'll return to the basecamp online portal to fill out an end-of-day report that details all of the assignments I've worked on, what I was able to complete, and my overall progress. This report helps not only my boss know what I was able to accomplish, but what my team members can expect from me over the next few days."

Over the last year, as Poliana hit the $1 million revenue mark, Rija has been at the forefront of Polianas internal marketing, bringing in new deals with better margins using amazing marketing.

After getting to talk with both John and Rija, it's clear to see that they are a perfect match. To this day, Rija is a marketing associate for John, aiming to become the future marketing director.

How a Sales Development Rep Closed 92 Deals

REPSTACK CASE STUDY

HOW A SALES DEVELOPMENT REP CLOSED 92 DEALS

JOSH NELSON | HENRY ADAMS

The next case study covers how one sales development representative closed over 92 deals in under three months. Henry went from an appointment setter to a sales executive in just a year and a half. His journey has been remarkable, and his results were astonishing as he was given more responsibilities. This is a perfect example of how an entry-level associate is soon moved into a management position.

It all started when Josh Nelson, agency owner of one of the fastest-growing companies in the Inc 5000, was looking for an appointment setter. He's had a great experience working with our sweet hustler, Henry Adams.

Josh Nelson is the guru and founder of the famous Seven Figure Agency. When I partnered Henry with Josh, Henry began mostly focusing on setting appointments for the sales manager that would lead to five-figure deals. It takes a whole new kind of self-confidence to make that promise.

What Josh discovered is that Henry is made of tougher material than others. He was able to impress the great Josh Nelson with his hard work and dedication. With a clean accent & perfect grammar, astute work ethic, and practical sense of client retention, Henry has made Mr. Nelson very happy. Henry is still a #1 RepStack associate today.

"

We at RepStack couldn't be more proud of how Henry demonstrates how to be a reliable virtual associate.

"

"We at RepStack couldn't be more proud of how Henry demonstrates how to be a reliable virtual associate." This is what Josh had to say personally about his sales assistant, with whom he's been working since December 2020. Josh added, "Henry, thank you. You're crushing it! You are such a great addition to our team. We appreciate you so much."

"You're doing a great job cranking away on the phones doing discovery calls. Following up with clients on HighLevel to book strategy session appointments to help grow the business."

It is clear that Josh is very pleased with Henry's work and how it is helping to grow the agency. Henry has been moved into a management position where he gets to close big deals. It shows that a virtual associate is not a temporary team member but someone who is responsible and able to take on more tasks as they continue to learn more.

Curious about how Henry was able to grow so fast from an appointment setter to a sales executive in a short amount of time, I held a video call with him to see what his secret recipe was.

He explained, "On a daily basis, I will take both outbound and inbound calls using HighLevel. As soon as I log on for the day, I'm ready to assist prospective clients with learning more. I have a good script to use, but I can always be flexible based on how the conversation is going, so I don't sound like a robot. I want to be someone whom the prospective client can have an intelligent conversation with.

"Besides that, I'm calling each prospective client in the funnel to see if they are interested in setting up a strategy session. If a client is interested in setting up a strategy session, he moves them into his strategy session tracking sheet.

"In the last three months, I've made 3000 calls. Five hundred of those clients picked up the phone, and 92 of them led to five-figure deals.

"When it's all said and done, I complete a day-end report to show how many calls I've received or made, and of those calls how many are leading to bookings."

Henry started out as an appointment setter and now is a sales executive with Josh Nelson. If you bring in the right person, they will take on more responsibilities and team members underneath them.

If you want someone to change the game for you and still allow you to keep your budget, then working with a virtual associate is the solution that you need.

Account Manager Case Study: Asmaa

REPSTACK CASE STUDY

ACCOUNT MANAGER CASE STUDY: ASMAA

LYN ASKIN | ASMAA KHAN

Lyn Askin, the CEO of Raxxar Digital Marketing, has experienced excellence while working with his account manager, Asmaa.

Though this company focuses on web development for clients in Louisiana, they also create marketing campaigns for global clients based on their industry. This agency's main goal is to help its clients increase their revenue through digital platforms. They also get to help countless other digital marketing agencies, too.

When he brought on his new account manager, I was interested to hear his thought on having this new associate on his team. Since Asmaa joined their team, Lyn has seen incredible growth in the company. He describes her as follows, "She's been amazing so far. She's done everything we've asked and is eager to learn. She's proactive, which makes us excited to have her as part of the team. I am certainly looking forward to growing with her because I appreciate her so much."

Lyn is clearly delighted to have Asmaa as part of the team because she is eager to learn, she's proactive, and she is making sure her work is organized and prioritized.

When I was able to catch up with Asmaa to see how she's been doing in her new position, she had a lot of positive things to say. She's looking forward to being with the company for years to come. Since she began working with Raxxar as an account manager, she described to me the things she'd been doing.

She said, "I'm acting as a liaison between the client and departments within the agency to convey information, ensure understanding, and make certain everything gets done in an accurate, timely manner."

"I really enjoy managing the team and delegating tasks that lead to greater success for the agency. I'm making sure all of the projects, with their many parts, are being completed on a tight schedule."

"What I also enjoy is getting to develop strong relationships with customers. I think building those relationships is very important for the future success of the agency.

"Throughout the day, I'm in contact with my team members through Slack. I'll review the emails, reply to them, or complete any tasks associated with new emails from the agency's current clients. I'll also check all the emails through Help Scout to be up-to-date with all of Raxxar's clients." "With those new tasks, I'll communicate with the team on Team Works, posting the new tasks to which the team members will be assigned. In addition, I'll create the new projects on Team Works for all of the new Raxxar clients."

"As content is being created, I'll review all the content submitted by the team members."

"Right now, I am managing monthly press releases for 20 SEO clients. I have to update all tracking sheets for clients and current projects."

Asmaa is a true asset to her team because she is hard-working and can stay organized even when there are many projects happening simultaneously. Asmaa's taking on this role has freed up Lyn to focus on the growth of his agency.

Becoming The Free Agency Owner

After reading through these case studies, can you imagine what your life would be like if you had these three virtual associates working for you? You'd be able to live a stress-free life knowing that the most vital day-to-day tasks were being taken care of by trusted individuals you are going to stick with for the long term.

When you step back and let go of managing every aspect of your agency, you will be able to open your eyes to all the possibilities for growth. This is called the growth mode when you've established these three key roles in your agency.

You already know that a better, freer life is possible. You've seen plenty of other marketing agency owners live wonderful lives. Now you are starting to discover the secret to how they are able to gain that freedom while still running their $1 million agencies.

As you progress through the rest of this book, you'll not only come to understand these three key roles but when is the perfect time to hire these individuals. More so, you'll be given the perfect job placement ads that you can use right away to find the best candidates.

"

It's important to note that there is a precise time to bring into the team a marketing assistant, sales development rep, and account manager.

"

It's important to note that there is a precise time to bring a marketing assistant, sales development rep, and account manager into the team. They need to be hired in this order and only when you have other systems in place. As you continue reading this book, you'll discover what those systems are and how they can help you automate your agency.

Everything you ever dreamed about when you started your digital marketing agency can happen. It did for me when I learned to delegate my workload. Then I was able to operate my agency stress-free, knowing that I had put into place the key individuals that were going to ensure that my agency grew.

Now, not only do I manage over one hundred associates, but I've reached that $1 million a year mark. I plan to see that number increase in the years to come. We are already doing everything I talk about in this book at my agency, and many of our digital marketing agency clients are doing these things, too, to activate growth. You're going to learn how to do the same thing and understand why there is a particular process of doing so.

We will lay out all the options available to you in sourcing these people, whether you want to hire a virtual assistant, a virtual associate, or a local manager.

As you dive into the answer to hiring for these three key roles in the next chapter, you'll get to understand the importance of each of these three individuals, depending on where you are inside your agency journey and how each role fits in and plays its part. Until you understand the process, you won't experience the growth mode our clients and we have been experiencing.

You're about to learn that secret!

Chapter 3:

The Answer, Hire For 3 Key Roles

In the beginning years of my digital marketing agency, I struggled with wearing so many hats. I was used to calling 10-20 clients a day. I would have to juggle onboarding new clients while creating my own prospect list. Then I would have to switch back to marketing. It was a real struggle every day, a struggle that you are no doubt very familiar with.

But that struggle vanished when I stumbled upon my company idea for RepStack. I was able to help countless agencies grow on a massive scale by identifying and implementing 3 key roles. It happens when you're able to create an internal marketing department, an internal sales department, and an internal customer service department. These are the cornerstones for any digital marketing agency that wants to move away from a mom-and-pop shop and become a true agency.

You can start a digital marketing agency with little to no money. That is why most agency owners choose this route versus offering coding services. Digital marketing has a lower threshold than other digital start-ups.

Agency owners come from all sorts of different backgrounds. Some are nerds and like design, coding, etc. Others are like me with experience in sales but need help on the design and development side of digital marketing.

Most marketing agency owners have some sort of sales background before they decide to open up shop. They are experts in their industry and understand how to best market in their chosen niche based on those years of experience.

I started my digital market agency as a side hustle, wanting to break away from the normal 9-5 job and achieve the success I had dreamed about. I understood how to sell based on my years working in sales at BestBuy. I also knew how to work well with others.

But when I started making a six-figure income, I was being stretched thin doing it all alone. I didn't have any employees, and there were times when I didn't even have partners in the agency.

I always wanted to build a million-dollar agency, but I just could not move forward, no matter how hard I worked.

At one point in 2020, I decided to get a business coach, and that started to turn things around fast.

With the help of my coach, I discovered the three key roles for agency growth. Hiring these three key roles turned everything around for me. What I learned; I want you to be able to learn as well. Below are some of the main things I learned from my mentor.

With your marketing agency, you are offering a wide range of services in your niche.

- Website development
- SEO
- Facebook ads
- Google ads
- Automations through CRM (lead management system for clients)

In your agency, you are working with different outsourcing team members to meet all the needs of your clients. You have experience working with:

- Facebook team members who build ads, make creatives and content with graphic design, and who do video editing.
- Google ads specialist
- SEO team
- Website designer and developer
- Automation specialist
- Project manager

These are the basics for any marketing agency and the ones owners will usually hire first. But while these may be the pieces and parts that make fulfilling a client's request possible, there are much larger moving parts that make a marketing agency successful.

The tasks that most agency owners do on their own include:

- Doing some sort of marketing activity to pull the clients in.
- Conducting discovery calls or strategy sessions.
- Setting up strategy appointments to sell services.
- Managing client projects from beginning to end. Being an account manager.

DOING MARKETING ACTIVITIES

CONDUCTING DISCOVERY CALLS

SELL SERVICES

MANAGE CLIENT PROJECTS

No longer are you working the 9-5 job, but you've come to realize that managing your own marketing agency requires almost twelve-hour days to do it all. These tasks often take up an entire day's work and more. Especially the way you are running things right now.

But that's not how you become successful. That's how you become burnt out. You'll start to wonder why you even decided to get into this business in the first place.

Identifying these three key roles was a game-changer for me. And even though most agency owners don't initially think of hiring for these positions, this is undoubtedly the cornerstone of every successful agency in the world right now. The said positions include the marketing associate, sales development representative, and account manager. Identifying these roles is like laying the first brick in the foundation of your agency.

Eventually, the people in these roles will become team leads, and you will begin to grow your marketing, sales, and accounts departments with additional employees.

"

These three positions, in a particular hiring order, leads a marketing agency into growth mode.

"

These three positions, in a particular hiring order, lead a marketing agency into growth mode. They take care of the daily grind that you are often bogged down with. Instead of being stressed out every day about your workload, you can put your trust in an individual who is going to do it for you and save you money in the long run.

This is how you move from being a stuck agency owner to a free agency owner. You will have more free time to do the things that are really important to you—growing your agency and strengthening meaningful relationships, spending time on vacation, and not always grinding for growth. I struggled with the same problems many agency owners face. As I searched for better solutions, I found that these 3 strategic roles play a big part inside my agency. Thanks to these individuals, who I call virtual associates, I can take a step back and hand over the workload. I went from stuck to stumbling across the obvious magic of hiring 3 key roles, and now I work with 100+ agencies. I've proved that my hunch was right.

Today, I have a great team of virtual associates who all work remotely. Many agency owners can relate to the fact that most of your team members are scattered across the world. Skilled talent can be found in any country, and when your virtual associates are accustomed to international time zones, the sky's the limit when it comes to agency growth.

My agency is a perfect example. Although we're based in Pakistan, the associates of RepStack are actively opening up new markets all over the globe because the demand for our services is extremely high.

When I was first finding solutions for my marketing agency, I was scouring the internet to find reliable help. This would lead me through a whole new process of how to find reliable virtual associates. I have completely opened new hiring grounds.

As I hired fulfillment partners for my digital marketing agency, I became familiar with online job posting websites such as Fiverr and Upwork. Their platforms allow you to find freelancers with a wide variety of specialty skills. What makes these freelancers persuasive to work with is that they are very cost-effective, with average fees starting at as little as $4 an hour. This can make you think that you could save a lot of money working with a freelancer.

> *There is a larger difference between working with a part-time freelancer who is a virtual assistant compared to working with a dedicated virtual worker.*

However, there is a larger difference between working with a part-time freelancer who is a virtual assistant compared to working with a dedicated virtual worker.

I learned the hard way when the freelancers I was hiring would not provide the same quality they were advertising or would disappear altogether halfway through the project. I discovered that it was very hard to find reliable freelancers who could provide excellent services.

Finding the right person who will do a great job will help your agency grow faster.

Later in this book, you'll get the tools you need to place hiring ads. These ads will get you the quality virtual associates you need to become a great success. It's time for you to enter growth mode for your agency by hiring these three key roles.

Your Agency Journey

I'm sure you're excited to get started searching for the perfect virtual associates for your agency. And while it's important to understand that these three key roles need to be hired in a particular order, what's more important is that each role depends on where you are inside your agency journey.

I've always loved sales and talking to people, but it's also fun growing your agency. In order to grow your agency, of course, you need to land clients. Therefore, you need to develop some sort of system to gain clients. For my team members, we look at sales as fun. For the majority of our clients, we use the familiar two-step process that begins with discovery calls that are then booked for a strategy session. After reviewing the client's website, the sales team will do a full demo with the prospective client on the second call.

This is a fantastic process that my sales development representatives can easily implement and crush each day.

But if you don't have a process like this already in place, then your agency isn't ready for a sales development rep. Instead, you'd first need to start with a marketing associate to build your prospect list and give your future sales development rep someone to call and sell to.

With an automated process like this in place, you, as the agency owner, no longer need to focus on those sales calls. It's a great feeling to sit back and let someone else sell for me. Instead, I get to see the new sales orders coming in because of the systems I've already implemented. As you think about where you are in your agency journey, you have to decide if you have the systems in place where a virtual associate would be able to join your team, learn the system, and get right to work. Each of the three key roles plays an important part in growing your agency, but it won't happen if you don't have any systems in place.

"

If you are currently only making $10-20k a month, you are still in the freelance part of your journey.

"

If you are currently only making $10-20k a month, you are still in the freelance part of your journey. You might be comfortable only making $10k a month. But for most digital marketing agency owners, you want to make more. You don't want to be considered a freelancer but a reputable agency that provides solutions.

If you're looking to:

- Grow and create a seven-figure agency
- To hire team members to create a really unique company
- To become an entrepreneur and build other companies

Importance of Training and Development

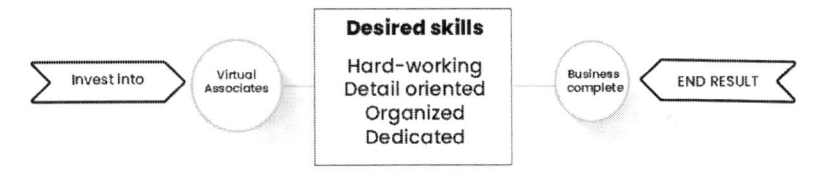

Invest into → Virtual Associates → **Desired skills**: Hard-working, Detail oriented, Organized, Dedicated → Business complete → END RESULT

You need to start investing in yourself. That means that you're going to gain the knowledge you need to become a success (just like you are doing right now with this book). You can't achieve your dreams until you discover the road to getting to where you want to be.

As you invest in yourself and your skill set, you'll discover how to put into practice certain systems and roles in your agency that will help you reach the seven-figure mark. Those are the key elements of growth you will gain from this book.

All successful companies around the world invest in their employees. As you begin the process of hiring these three key roles, be prepared to train these individuals to work through your systems just like you would. Though many virtual associates already have many desired skills such as hard-working, detailed-oriented, organization, and dedication, they still need to learn how you'll like to have your business run.

As agency owners continue to do all the work themselves, they, in turn, become their own bottlenecks. There are better ways to manage many of the functions you are used to tackling each day.

To get the number of sales you are dreaming of each month, you'll need to be able to step back and hand over some of these tasks to virtual associates.

Once you discover where you are in your agency journey, you'll be able to spot places that need to be filled by a virtual associate. Each of these three key roles fits into the working mechanics of your business. Now, these three key roles are going to play a major part in growing your agency.

Marketing Associate

While most agency owners who want to put their company into growth mode first think of working with a sales development rep, it is actually the marketing associate that should be initially hired to kick start growth mode.

RIGHT ORDER OF HIRING FOR 3 KEY ROLES

1. Marketing Associate
2. Sales Development Rep
3. Account Manager

Until you have a marketing associate on your team, you will always wonder how you're going to get your agency's name in front of new clients. Once you put someone in this virtual role, a person who will be putting 40 hours a week into this task, you'll see how fast everyone will see your agency.

This is one of three key roles that will put your agency into growth mode. And it's the first one that needs to be implemented so the other two can succeed.

Remember, marketing isn't going to equal dollars to days. But it will grow your agency in the future when your prospect can find you on YouTube and see a variety of marketing material on social media.

If you're not doing marketing for your agency on an ongoing basis, you won't be able to feed the sales engine. You've already experienced what it feels like to jump back and forth between marketing and sales to make revenue.

Once you've filled the position of marketing associate on your team, your key campaigns and funnels will be running at full speed. Once they can create the marketing campaigns and get them running, you'll be targeting prospects 24/7.

If you are still wondering whether you need a marketing associate, here are the top five reasons to hire for this key role:

> YOU WANT TO FREE UP TIME TO STEP BACK FROM THE DAY-TO-DAY TASK OF CREATING MARKETING CAMPAIGNS

1. **You want to free up time to be able to step back from the day-to-day task of creating marketing campaigns.** A marketing associate can perform your core activities, allowing you to have more time to focus on growing your business.

2. **You want to reduce overhead costs while growing your agency.** Most agency owners hire marketing associates to lower their overhead costs. When marketing associates create funnels that bring in five-figure deals, it offsets their salary of $30k a year.

3. **You want to quickly scale your agency's operations.** A marketing associate takes on the role of creating content and marketing campaigns, which will increase all the other mechanics of your agency.

4. **You want to strengthen this weak part of your agency**. A marketing assistant can fill the gap in your agency by providing a pipeline of extra skill sets.

5. **You want someone available 24/7**. You often rely on your own skills and time to fulfill your agency's marketing needs. Step back and let someone else tackle these tasks while working in international time zones and on weekends. You have your marketing associate to step in for you even when you are unavailable.

The marketing department's goal should be to hand over 15-20 discovery calls every single month so that sales can close 2-5 deals out of those booked discovery calls.

The marketing associate plays a key role for your agency and can help to continue the marketing engine on an ongoing basis without breaks. This person will report back to you or the marketing manager with all their daily tasks to show their achievements.

Some of their tasks can include:

- Managing cold outreach campaigns.
- Take care of your social media profiles and post regular updates.
- Oversee time launch and manage paid ad campaigns.
- Manage the CRM system to assist the sales and marketing teams.
- Build funnels and put them into place.

[CONTENT CREATION] [BUILD PROCESSES]

[PAID ADVERTISING]

[COLD OUTREACH] [MANAGE CRM]

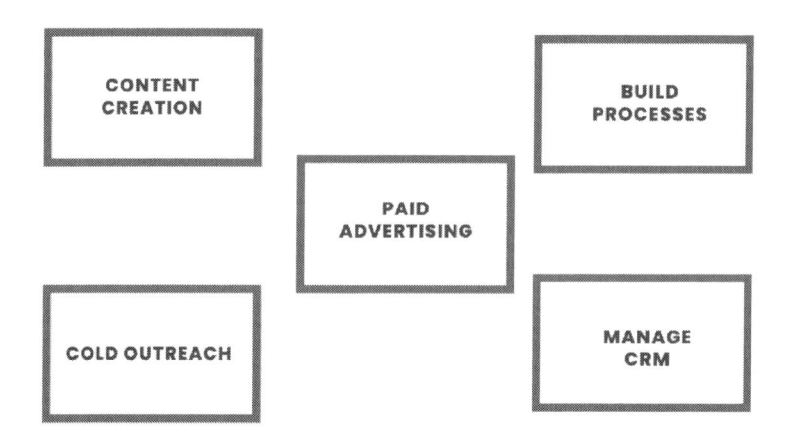

As you read through that list, you no doubt have several thoughts running through your mind. The first is that this represents the type of daily work you're used to doing as a one-man band. And second, the idea of how much free time you'd have when you hire for this position.

Before you place an ad to hire a marketing associate, one of your tasks is to make a list of all your goals as an agency owner. This includes hiring a marketing associate who will produce 15-20 discovery calls each month.

Use that list as part of your interview process when you start hiring for this position. Determine if the potential marketing associate will be able to perform those tasks and do them better than you've been able to do thus far. We all continue to learn and grow each day. You'll be surprised at what an experienced marketing associate can do for you and what you can learn from them.

A good marketing associate should have identified their niche, established a lead list, and created a strong outreach campaign. Using the list of goals you made for your agency, make sure you prioritize it for your marketing associate. For example, if you've been struggling to post more than one social media post on your platforms, have your marketing associate post new content three times a week.

> *Being a successful agency owner isn't about being perfect. It's about making progress.*

Being a successful agency owner isn't about being perfect. It's about making progress. When you are focusing on completing work for your agency, you need to delegate important tasks to other trusted individuals. You'll watch your agency grow when you hand over those tasks to a marketing associate.

That is why hiring a marketing associate should be the first key role you seek for your agency.

Sales Development Representative

Once you have your marketing associate in place, it's time to consider implementing the next of the three key roles – sales development representative. Just like a marketing associate, adding a sales development representative to your team will take your agency to the next level. While you may have all the content team members and SEO specialists on board, it's important to take the time to implement a team member who can focus purely on sales. There is normally a two-part sales mechanism that most agency owners we work with use. The first part is making discovery calls, and the second is scheduling strategy sessions.

Discovery calls are booked calls that have been transferred to the sales department. Those can be a wide range of calls, from cold calls to emails and messages on social media. These can be potential clients who have entered into a funnel or lead magnet created by the marketing associate. During discovery calls, a sales development rep assesses a client's needs, and the current status of their business is discussed. Next, you let the client know if they qualify to work with your agency and if so, a strategy session is scheduled to discuss pricing and a marketing plan to help increase the client's business.

In today's modern era, reaching potential clients is how an agency continues to grow. You often find yourself sending emails and responding to social media messages more than you are calling clients. From your marketing team, you'll find that they are reaching clients on several different platforms, from Facebook to YouTube.

You rely on a team of individuals who specialize in creating engaging content to capture your potential clients in order to funnel them into a contact list. Now, it's time to put an individual into the spot you have been focusing on for so long.

While you might think at first that it's important for the agency owner to make contact with all prospective clients, that's going to be a waste of your precious time. You are an expert, and your time is very valuable. Instead, focus on making strong connections with current clients.

> "WHILE YOU MIGHT THINK AT FIRST THAT IT'S IMPORTANT FOR THE AGENCY OWNER TO MAKE CONTACT WITH ALL PROSPECTIVE CLIENTS, THAT'S GOING TO BE A WASTE OF YOUR PRECIOUS TIME"

The job of a sales development rep is being able to call on all the leads in his marketing funnel, monitor the website optics that come in, make sure appointments are booked, schedule strategy sessions, and eventually be able to close a deal.

Imagine having that sales development rep who is working eight hours a day, 40 hours a week, 160 hours a month. They are then able to make 80-100 calls, emails, or messages a day while you can focus solely on meeting with interested clients in a strategy session.

If you love sales or at least love talking with interested clients to seal the deal, let the sales development rep get those clients to you by doing the daily grind. They can even follow up with clients who ask to call them back on another day. You are then able to focus solely on strategy sessions.

One of the biggest things a sales development rep can offer you is peace of mind. When you are a busy entrepreneur stomping out fires, it's reassuring to know that at the end of the week, a certain number of calls, emails, and messages went out. In turn, a certain number of leads came in, as several clients signed up through your website. You can place your trust in your sales development rep to grab that information, call them back, and arrange a time for that client's calendar to be able to sit down for a strategy call.

Instead of jumping around with all these different tasks, you can delegate them to a sales development rep who will focus only on these tasks. That is how you put your agency into growth mode.

Think about all the times you forgot to call a client back because you're being pulled in so many directions. That could have been a hot lead that would have produced a five-figure deal.

Since you forgot to call them back during the scheduled time, it's a cold lead, or they've booked with someone else.

This is why a sales development rep is so important and gives you great peace of mind.

An overview of what a sales development rep can do includes:

- Proactively sets sales appointments for the director of business development.
- Follow up with inbound leads.
- Reaches out to prospect lists by calling, emailing, texting, and social media messaging.

- Calls are initiated via your CRMs (HighLevel, HubSpot, etc.), so there is an accurate log of activity, and calls are recorded.

- All scheduled discovery calls and strategy sessions are then set using your calendar link.

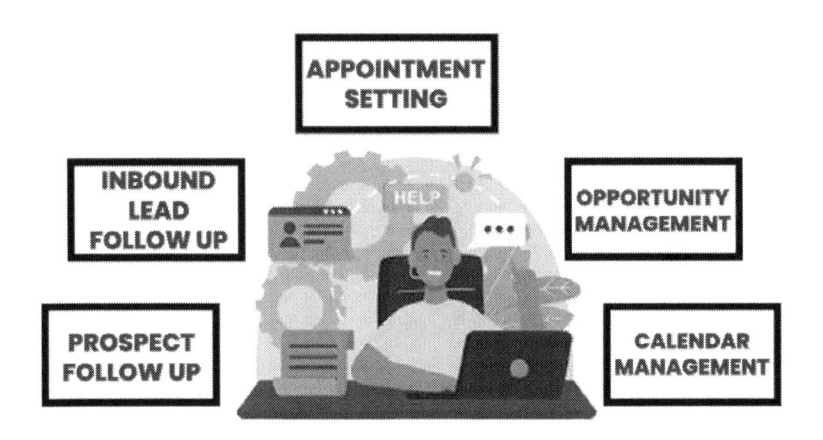

Take the time to visualize what the future holds for your agency. Think of all the possibilities for growing your agency when you have a dedicated individual taking care of all these tasks. What would that mean for you and your agency when you have these tasks taken care of 40 hours a week?

You're beginning to discover just how important these 3 key roles are for your agency and how it puts your business into serious growth mode. The $1 million mark doesn't seem like a pipe dream any longer.

Account Manager

Now that you have your marketing and sales development reps in place, you're going to need an account manager.

Now that you have your marketing and sales development reps in place, you will need an account manager.

With the first of the three key roles in place, you will see an increase in clients. You and your team will provide solutions to clients who want to market their business digitally. You'll also have several teams to make sure these solutions are created in a timely manner. You'll have the social media team create content, post content, and edit videos.

You'll have SEO specialists.

You'll have web designers and developers.

In a nutshell, you're going to have several teams to take care of every aspect of the project that the client wants to be done.

But you have a choice. You can either manage all of these teams yourself, falling into the pitfall of micromanaging and taking away your precious time. Or, you can hire the last of the three key roles: account manager. With these three key roles in place, your agency is going to run on autopilot. The only thing you're going to do is meet with your clients to upsell them or perhaps just focus on marketing your own business to get in front of more clients. When you are able to step back from overseeing all of your clients, you will be surprised by how much free time you now have on your hands.

> *No matter what you want to be spending your time doing, having an account manager as part of your team is going to help you get there*

No matter what you want to spend your time doing, having an account manager as part of your team will help you get there faster. This is a team member that is going to handle and manage your current clients. They will assist your current accounts by providing support from the beginning to the end of their projects. And on top of that, they will lead and manage all of your internal teams. Every agency owner struggles with letting go of account management. You might feel that you need to be there for every part of the project. You need to be in constant contact with your other teams to ensure that the project is being completed on time and the way the client wants it to be done.

You feel that you need to reply or call back a client as soon as they reach out to you because maybe you closed the deal or you know them personally. But when you start to get more than ten clients, you will need someone else to manage each of these clients for you.

Here is a list of tasks and traits that you'll find in an account manager:

- They are excellent communicators with a commitment to client satisfaction.
- They thrive in an account management position since they are normally extroverts and highly organized.
- They are attentive to the needs of the clients to ensure happy customers who maintain long-term relationships with the agency.
- They are the liaison between clients and the cross-functioning internal teams to ensure timely and successful delivery of the client's solutions.
- They manage and develop client accounts to initiate and maintain favorable relationships.
- They also lead a team of account managers dedicated to meeting their assigned clients' operational needs by upselling and growing testimonials.

As you can see, account managers are the virtual associates that tie the entire agency together. They oversee the agency's daily operations and will go as far as replying to all the emails and calls you are receiving from your clients.

While this chapter gave an overview of the three key roles that will put your agency into growth mode, the following chapters will dive deeper into these roles. You'll not only learn how to place the best job posts to get high-quality virtual associates, but you'll be given a deeper understanding of how they'll fit into your agency.

Chapter 4:

Secret #1: The First Brick in The Foundation, The Marketing Associate

There is a particular order in which the three key roles must be implemented into your agency. You can't onboard a sales development rep if you don't have any clients for that individual to call. That is why to start growth mode for your agency and stir up interest in your business, you have to start with a rock star of a marketing associate.

This is the first person on your internal marketing team. With this first brick, you're building that growth machine for the agency.

In this chapter, you will get a breakdown of this essential role and how it will save you time and money. You will be able to talk to a trusted individual about many of the processes you're doing right now for marketing, from developing content to running ad campaigns. While this chapter focuses on this first secret unlocked, the next chapter will give details on how to discover a quality marketing associate, the hiring process, as well as their onboarding process. For now, you'll get the knowledge of all that a marketing associate can do for you and the solutions they can provide.

You already have several teams in place for your agency—members who focus on social media content and ads, web developers and SEO specialists. Now it's time to start putting your marketing team in place.

> *Now it's time to start putting your marketing team in place as well.*

A marketing associate plays the anchor role in kickstarting your agency's growth. In order to get new clients for your agency, you have to get your name out in front of them. Not only are you competing against other marketing agencies, but against all other advertisements found in the same space you are launching your ad campaigns.

Having key campaigns and funnels in place for your agency is the first part of building your marketing team.

▶ **LAUNCH KEY CAMPAIGNS**

▶ **SOCIAL MEDIA MANAGEMENT**

▶ **SETTING UP & MANAGING YOUR CRM**

▶ **LEAD GENERATION**

▶ **LAUNCH AND MANAGE PODCASTS/WEBINARS**

In the first six months, the marketing associate should be completely focused on marketing the agency and getting the agency's information out there and set up correctly. For 160 hours a month, they will focus on core outreach campaigns, cleaning up the lead list, and doing it full-time. Their sole purpose is to successfully book 15-20 calls for the sales team every month.

The goal is to become a free agency owner – a person who is able to step back and watch their agency blossom without needing to manage every aspect of it.

By putting a marketing associate into place, they can accomplish key essential campaigns such as identifying niche markets, building a quality list of prospects, launching and optimizing cold outreach campaigns, and, if budget allows, launching paid ad campaigns on Facebook and Google. They can also coordinate syndication of social media content and create podcasts and webinars for owners.

If you don't have these key campaigns and funnels already set up with a marketing plan for your agency, it will be difficult to grow your business. Therefore, relying on a marketing associate to help you launch and optimize these key campaigns is not only going to save you time but is also the first step towards unlocking seven-figure revenues for your agency.

To begin really unlocking growth, have a roadmap in place for your marketing associate and have them begin implementing the essential campaigns as soon as possible.

Working with a company like RepStack, which provides blueprints of tried and tested ways of marketing success for agency owners, cuts down the growth trajectory. You must have a plan from day one, so that the new marketing manager can come in and start implementing it immediately.

RepStack Agency Growth Tracks
The OnRamp Program – Powered by Seven Figure Agency

Marketing Agency Growth Tracks

Agency Marketing Blueprint

Business Model Fundamentals
- BMF Introduction
- Choose Your Model
- Goals & Targets
- Recommended Tools & Startup Costs

The Landing Clients Model

1. Decide Niche
1.1 Decide Niche Introduction
1.2 Conduct Research & Choose Niche
1.3 Module Summary

2. Map Your Program
2.1 Map Your Program Introduction
2.2 Decide Service Offering
2.3 Build Program Overview
2.4 Create Fulfillment Plan
2.5 Map Your Program Summary

3. Establish Positioning
3.1 Establish Positioning Introduction
3.2 Setup Baseline Positioning
3.3 Setup Your Appointment Funnel
3.4 Establish Online Presence
3.5 Setup Your Checklist Lead Magnet & Funnel
3.6 Module Summary

Landing Clients – Your KEY Focus

4. Get List
4.1 Get The List Introduction
4.2 Sphere Of Influence
4.3 Buy List
4.4 Scrape List (Don't)
4.5 Join The Association
4.6 Get The List Summary

5. Start Outreach
5.1 Cold Outreach Introduction
5.2 Cold Outreach Strategy Overview
5.3 Setup Your HighLevel Account For Cold Outreach
5.4 Setup The Outreach Campaigns & Workflow
5.5 Run The One City Outreach Strategy
5.6 Other Outreach Campaigns & Angles
5.7 Cold Outreach Summary

6. Work The Pipeline
6.1 Work The Pipeline Introduction
6.2 How To Work The Pipeline
6.3 Sending Value Videos
6.4 Work The Pipeline Summary

Agency Sales Blueprint

Sales Process Overview

7. Discovery Call
7.1 Discovery Call Intro
7.2 How To Run A Discovery Call
7.3 Disocvery Call Summary

8. Meeting Prep
8.1 Meeting Prep Intro
8.2 How To Run Reports & Prepare for Meeting
8.3 Meeting Prep Summary

9. Strategy Session
9.1 Strategy Session Introduction
9.2 How To Conduct A Strategy Session
9.3 Sales Process Management
9.4 Strategy Session Summary

Hot Lead Follow Up is a combination of both Marketing & Sales

10. Hot Lead Follow Up
10.1 Hot Lead Follow Up Introduction
10.2 Setting Up Your Hot Lead Follow Up
10.3 Hot Lead Follow Up Summary

RepStack X SEVEN FIGURE AGENCY

The process of gaining new clients starts with having a good marketing team. A good marketing team has the capacity to capture those prospective clients to convert them into new customers. Once you have this in place, you'll be able to step back and watch your agency grow with little effort on your part.

Getting Back To The Basics

As I often say, agency owners have to eat their own dog food. What I mean by this is that for every strategy you offer your clients, you must first have your own solid marketing plan in place to see your agency grow.

Therefore, it's important to get back to the basics, have a blueprint in place for your marketing associate, work with a marketing coach or agency like RepStack, and ensure that your key campaigns and funnels are in place before you consider hiring a marketing associate.

Having a marketing plan is vital to the growth of your own agency. When you have a marketing plan in place, your marketing associate will be able to review it and quickly get to work. If you don't have a plan, your new marketing associate is going to struggle to complete the tasks that you want with little direction. The basics of marketing, as you are probably very familiar with, is that you need to have a message (what) in order to appeal to the market (who) and how you're going to get in front of that market, media (how).

```
        WHO
    CENTRE-BASICS
     OF MARKETING
  WHAT          HOW
```

You'll also need to prioritize the media you will use to appeal to your target audience. Though a marketing associate can handle several types of marketing tasks, you'll need to explain to this team member which tasks are most important and which ones will have the *greatest effect* on your target audience. A new team member will need a solid leader to follow.

Completing a marketing strategy session with yourself will set you up for success when you hire a marketing associate.

> *Understanding your niche, your audience, and the most important media you want to use will make the onboarding process much faster for your new team member*

Understanding your niche, your audience, and the most important media you want to use will make the onboarding process much faster for your new team member. By doing so, your new marketing associate will be able to understand your agency and mission quickly. Then they'll be able to jump right on the tasks that you need to be completed first before creating possible new media in the future.

This can be a quick activity if you have already put into place a marketing plan. You will enjoy this process, and you might even discover something new about your agency or the niche you are marketing to. If you don't already have a niche, this is the time to establish that.

Every marketing agency has a unique message. This message defines who you are, what you do, what makes you unique, and why someone should hire you rather than another business offering the same service.

Once you have your message, you specifically define your market. This is who you sell to and who your best customers are.

As you detail the characteristics of your target audience, ensure that it falls into a specific niche. You don't want to be marketing to the entire world, but to a specific target, so you always hit the bullseye.

Look at the media you'll use to appeal to your target audience to start generating leads and a solid list, such as pay-per-click ads, SEO, social media posts, direct mail, and more. That is the tactics you'll use. These become your daily tasks, and that's how you can reach the best customers. However, if you focus solely on the media or the tactics you want to use for your agency, you will likely fail regardless of how well-selected that media is. With that being said, you need to scale back to the fundamentals.

Invest the time and energy in fleshing out your message and truly understand who your market is. By doing so, all your media choices will be vastly more effective, you will have a solid list in the works, and you can begin launching campaigns.

When you have these three M's defined, then you're ready to hire a marketing associate.

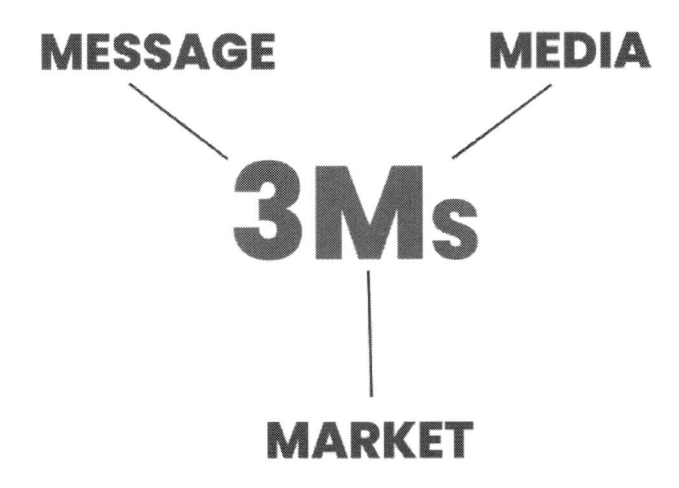

MESSAGE   **MEDIA**

3Ms

MARKET

Remember to be a good leader, set up your new marketing associate for success with a clear blueprint, and let them know the key things they should be doing.

The Marketing Associate Is The Anchor

The marketing associate is the first brick you need to become an agency. It is a key role for your agency because they are able to fuel your marketing engine on an ongoing basis without breaks. All agency owners eventually realize that they need a marketing associate to take over the daily operations.

BRICKS WITH MARKETING ASSOCIATE

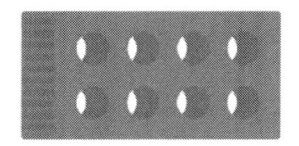

If you don't enjoy creating social media posts for all your platforms, then delegate that task. If you struggle with writing cold call scripts for your sales development reps, then rely on your marketing team to do that work for you.

Establishing your marketing associate is going to open up a world of possibilities. By incorporating this individual into your team, even if your agency is still starting out, they will anchor your entire agency in growth mode.

This means that you can't sell your services to a client who doesn't even know that you exist. And while cold calls are still a way to get your name out into the world, that sales tactic is becoming outdated with rising technology.

> *In order to be a successful marketing agency, you have to understand all the different ways to market yourself and your clients in the digital world*

In order to be a successful marketing agency, you have to understand all the different ways to market yourself and your clients in the digital world. You may have discovered the solutions for the majority of your target audience. They might need a better website, effective SEO, or a way to reach their target audience on social media. But are you doing the same thing for yourself? You must lead by example.

Having effective copywriting for your agency is important to start funneling clients into your key campaigns and funnels. While you might be able to source this work with a freelancer, it is another task a marketing associate can manage. Remember, think of the areas you struggle with, whether writing copy or developing a funnel to gather client contact information.

At this point, you should have a clear idea that you need a marketing associate on your team. Someone who can focus on all the different aspects of marketing to help your agency grow, just like the solutions you provide for other clients.

But you don't just want someone to take care of all of these tasks. You want to work with a marketing associate who adds value to your agency and your team.

- Someone who is enthusiastic about digital marketing.
- Has clear communication skills to work with all other team members.
- Already holds in-depth knowledge of digital marketing techniques.
- Excellent interpersonal skills.
- And able to work with strict deadlines.

Remember, you are looking to add a virtual associate to your team. Not just another virtual assistant.

> *A marketing associate is going to help your agency be anchored in growth mode*

A marketing associate is going to help your agency be anchored in growth mode. They will not just stick around for a few projects before moving on to another agency to work for. A marketing associate is a full-time team member ready to stick with you for the full life of your company.

When you start working with a marketing associate, you're going to see a vital shift in the daily operations of your agency. The daily tasks that used to weigh you down will be taken care of. Your key campaigns and funnels will start producing a larger prospect list for your sales team to follow up with.

The best part is that you will see the difference if you add a marketing associate to your team instead of trying to make projects work with freelancers and part-time employees. Working with someone who is dedicated to their tasks is a big game-changer.

A full-time marketing associate is often two steps ahead of you. When they come to you with a potential problem or bottleneck, they already have a list of solutions. All you have to do anymore is say yes or no to their ideas or possibly suggest a slight variation. The hassle of putting out fires has already been done for you.

"

The hassle of putting out fires has already been done for you".

"

These are the types of team members you will love working with: the marketing associate with the right type of attitude.

I know you'll be thinking right now about where you're going to find this individual who sounds more like a myth than reality. In the next chapter, I'll show you how to identify these key aspects and let you know how to post the right job ad to attract these individuals.

A Breakdown of the Marketing Associate Role

A marketing associate will be a multi-tasker, and they move fast. From graphic design to writing social media posts to basic video editing and posting on social media – any marketing task you can think of that you currently do; you can now delegate to a marketing associate. No task is too big or small to hand over to them with confidence; it will be completed, just like you would have done. A marketing associate can handle these tasks and more:

- Managing a lead marketing campaign on multiple social media platforms, including Facebook, Instagram, and LinkedIn.
- Creating Facebook ads.
- Google marketing campaigns.
- Emailing marketing campaigns.
- CRMs
- Supporting the marketing manager and marketing team with project organization.
- Performing administrative tasks to ensure the functionality of marketing activities.

- Conducting market research and analyzing marketing surveys.
- Employing online marketing analytics to gather information from the web and social media pages.
- Updating databases, spreadsheets, and inventory lists.
- Preparing promotional presentations and organizing promotional events.
- Composing and posting online content for the company's social media page and website.
- Writing marketing copy for company brochures and press releases.
- Building strong relationships with customers.
- Be willing to jump on the phone and make between 5-30 calls a day and book a discovery call for the sales team.

A marketing associate can initially work on the following campaigns/tasks:

1. Cold Outreach Campaigns
2. Social Media Outreach - LinkedIn and Facebook DM's
3. Launching Paid Ad Campaigns on Facebook, Google, etc.
4. Omnipresence through posting content on your social media
5. Webinar & Podcast setup/syndication

A MARKETING ASSOCIATE WORKS ON THE FOLLOWING TASKS

- PROSPECTING AND COLD OUTREACH CAMPAIGNS
- RUNNING PAID AD CAMPAIGNS
- CONTENT MANAGEMENT ACROSS YOUR SOCIAL MEDIA CHANNELS
- SETTING UP AND SYNDICATIONS OF PODCAST AND WEBINARS

Benchmarks You Should Expect

When you start working with a marketing associate, there are certain benchmarks you can expect to be met on a daily and weekly basis. After all, you will want to be able to see results right away with a marketing associate, even after their initial learning curve and how much they have learned about your particular agency.

What you are going for is seeing tangible results at the end of the month. You need a marketing associate who can produce results in a short amount of time to really boost your agency and put you in growth mode.

As you compare your last month's marketing reports to the current month, here are the benchmarks you can expect to see when you place a marketing associate on your team:

- Leads generated (combined marketing)
  * 5-10 a day
  * 25-50 per week
  * 100-200 per month
- Strategy calls booked from these leads:
  * 3-5 per week
  * 15 per month

BENCHMARKS EXPECTED FROM MARKETING ASSOCIATES

LEADS GENERATED (COMBINED MARKETING)
* 5-10 A DAY
* 25-50 PER WEEK
* 100-200 PER MONTH

STRATEGY CALLS BOOKED FROM THESE LEADS:
* 3-5 PER WEEK
* 15 PER MONTH

Can you imagine having 2-5 new retainer-based clients for your agency a month?

What kind of revenue could you expect for your agency and yourself with that type of workflow?

This is why the marketing associate is the anchor to the growth engine. By putting this individual on your team, you'll see the benchmarks above met monthly.

You'll not only be able to see your agency grow but your team size as well, as you start to onboard more employees that increase this growth.

With a marketing associate, you'll have wonderful days, brilliant weeks, and monumental months; you'll experience this month after month. As long as you follow the plan with your marketing associate, you will see the type of growth in your agency that you've only been able to dream about previously.

Over time, you'll be able to see these benchmarks grow. As your marketing associate becomes more familiar with your agency and is enthusiastic about your mission, you'll see these numbers grow steadily.

As you continue marching on, month after month, you will see your agency grow with these three key roles. To really be able to track these benchmarks, expect to receive an end-of-day report from your marketing associate and all other team members. By having these daily reports, you'll have tangible proof that your agency is growing.

Here are a few examples of the daily reports you can expect from your marketing associate:

Sample 1

Day end report (MM/DD/YYYY):

Hey Owner!

Here is the list of tasks that I got done today:
- Wrote content for the company's social media posts.
- Wrote content for the company and social media captions.
- Created 1 Animation post for the company's marketing and 1 Instagram Carousel post for the company's marketing.
- Did LinkedIn cold outreach program. Researched the people related to our niche, collected their information, and reached out to 40+ contacts.
- Wrote a blog post for the client on 8 treads for kids' fashion 2021.
- Published Posts on Facebook, LinkedIn, and Instagram for the company's marketing.
- Did hashtag research for organic boosting for the company.
- Designed 3-4 social media for the company and sent them for approval.
- Did LinkedIn cold outreach program for company marketing. Researched the people related to our niche,

collected their information, and reached out to 40+ contacts.
- Engaged with 10+ marketing Facebook groups that matched the company's niche on Facebook. Researched, found, and joined 3 groups related to our niche for Font marketing on LinkedIn.

Sample 2

Here's what I've been up to:
- Browsed through the company's folders to review the content we have to work with for social media & Google ads posting.
- Started reviewing the company's current performance (Facebook, FB ads, Instagram, etc.).
- Reviewed CCC's goal conversions from the past three months.
- Got the updated JKPS graphic and sent it over to the client.
- Coordinated with the designer and provided feedback for the Global Medical images for edits.
- Created a detailed action plan and suggestions for improving goal conversions for CCC and sent it to the client for review. Suggestions included simplifying forms, improving the mobile site, auditing the site for broken forms, etc.

- Continued working on the Interamerican Technical Institute campaign strategies for Facebook Ads and Google Ads.

- Edited the ITI Facebook Ads graphics and edited the text to fit Facebook's advertising standards.

- Searched Adobe Stock for vector images to replace two of the global medical graphics and sent them to the designer with instructions to update the images.

- Emailed the Interamerican graphics client for his review and feedback.

- Communicated with the designer regarding the updates from the first shoot day at GMTTI and offered to write up a demo script if needed.

- Continued working on brainstorming campaign strategies for the company's Facebook ads, Google ads, and social media marketing.

- Went through a social media marketing training course on Udemy.

These examples give a great peek into the daily life of a marketing associate. Reply to these reports to keep your associate busy working within the virtual environment. With these types of daily reports, you'll be able to track your agency's growth.

You'll also be able to step back from the daily grind of marketing your own agency and focus on the most important things in life – the type of freedom you've been dreaming about since you started your agency.

Case Study of a Marketing Associate

To really get a good idea of what you can expect from a marketing associate, the following case studies highlight what RepStack marketing associates have done for the clients they have been paired with. Use these as a standard as you prepare to read the next chapter, which focuses on how to hire a marketing associate.

REPSTACK CASE STUDY

CASE STUDY OF A MARKETING ASSOCIATE

OSCAR GURERRERO | RABBIYA

Case Study # 1

Oscar Guerrero is the agency owner of WeClick Group. To help grow his agency, he hired Rabbiya, a skilled marketing associate.

After just one month, this is what he had to say about Rabbiya.

"We had a huge growth in our company when we onboarded Rabbiya, and though I wasn't able to give her the attention she needed to learn more about the agency, she was able to help out in so many different ways without explicit guidance.

> *In our first month with Rabbiya on the team, we were able to secure three additional six-figure clients.*

In our first month with Rabbiya on the team, we were able to secure three additional six-figure clients. It was wonderful. In addition, the agency is getting a lot more exposure. She's handling my social media by posting all the videos I send her way. She is reaching our target audience, and we are definitely getting noticed.

"Because our marketing agency is getting noticed by even other competitors in my niche, we have been invited to a trade show I would have never known about if it hadn't been for Rabbiya's efforts on social media."

"It's been amazing to see what she is able to do with organic social media, and now as we prepare to launch Facebook ads, I have nothing but high expectations. In addition, she's going to start taking care of our cold emails as well."

From Oscar's testimony, you can clearly see the rising opportunities that are possible for agency owners when they add a marketing associate to their team. Not only are they able to handle everyday marketing tasks, but they are also able to open up the doors for new possibilities for the agency as a whole. With this type of growth, your agency will get to have all sorts of new experiences.

A brief overview of the tasks that Rabbiya completes for Oscar on a daily basis includes:

- Manage email campaigns on Woodpecker
- Manage social media posts, including creating them.
- Utilizes ClipScribe to create videos for social media.
- Uses Canva to create images for social media.
- Edits videos that are uploaded to the agency's YouTube channel.

At the end of the day, Rabbiya emails Oscar an end-of-day report that lists all the tasks she could complete for the agency in the marketing field. As Oscar delegates his marketing plan to Rabbiya, he's able to step back and focus on building stronger relationships with all his new clients.

REPSTACK CASE STUDY

WORKING WITH UME LAILA HAS BEEN FANTASTIC. LAILA IS JUST AMAZING

KEN TUCKER | UME LAILA

Case Study # 2

Ken Tucker is the founder of Changescape Web, a digital marketing agency that specializes in the niche of landscaping. When he was facing the challenge of appealing to his target niche, he hired Ume Laila as his marketing associate. This is what he had to say about his experience thus far.

"Working with Ume Laila has been fantastic. Laila is just amazing."

"

She's been able to pick up everything we've asked her to do and turn it around very quickly.

"

She's been able to pick up everything we've asked her to do and turn it around very quickly. It doesn't take a lot of oversight on my part to give her a task. And if she does need some help, she's very good at asking."

Ken's experience highlights the type of person you're looking for in a marketing associate – a go-getter like Laila, who comes to the client with a solution. But so, few virtual assistants possess the ability to be dedicated, enthusiastic, and not afraid to ask questions. Marketing associates have impeccable work ethics and can maintain clear communication on a daily basis.

With Changescape Web, Laila is the marketing solutions consultant. On a typical day, she often completes the following tasks:

- Clear and respond to all company emails.
- Uses Prospect Rocket (SEO tool) to monitor all marketing campaigns.
- Using Designrr, transcribes all podcasts from Ken before uploading them onto the agency's website.
- Creates social media and blog posts, then monitors their performance with Missinglettr.
- Creates lead campaigns and then uploads them to DFY Lead Team and Lead Kahuna to create prospect lists.
- Creates images for social media using Canva.
- Customizes videos using Invideo for social media uploading.
- Sends out a newsletter every Wednesday to contacts using Local Leads IQ.

Now you have seen what a marketing associate can do for you. In the next chapter, you'll be able to navigate the challenging task of hiring a marketing associate for your team.

Chapter 5:

Hiring, Onboarding, and Training your Marketing Associate

You will undergo a process to hire, onboard, and train your new marketing associate. It is a similar process for all three key roles. However, there are particular requirements you're going to be looking for in your new marketing assistant.

You have a few choices as you think about where you'd like to advertise for a marketing associate. You can use websites like Upwork and Fiverr, hoping to find a freelancer with experience who can be committed long term or work with a company such as RepStack that pairs marketing agency owners with trained and reliable virtual associates.

Another option is to use services like LinkedIn to find marketing associates who are more experienced and professional. In addition, you can advertise in the city you reside in to find local talent.

No matter which option you choose, you will be given the tools to post a successful help-wanted ad for a marketing associate in this chapter. Then you'll learn about our onboarding process that will ensure you are successful with your new employee.

Finally, you'll be given the direction on how to train your new team member using the important blueprints you have in place, so they can start attracting new clients for you right away.

By following this method of hiring, onboarding, and training your marketing associate, you'll set your agency up for success and enter that growth mode.

Job Descriptions

Once you decide which website(s) you will use to post a job description to create a pool of possible candidates, you have to construct your job description to attract the right marketing associate.

Below are two examples of a job description perfect for a marketing associate. As you review them, start thinking about how you'd customize one of them to fit your agency's main aim and objectives. Remember, you're not just hiring another virtual assistant. You're preparing to hire a marketing associate that is going to be with you for a long-term position.

Example One

Digital Marketing Virtual Associate

We're looking for someone who can take over the role of a Marketing Associate for our Digital Marketing Agency *Agency Name*

This position requires someone with leadership skills, excellent interpersonal skills, and a fast-paced learner with a coachable personality who can work in the ***Time Zone* time zone**. This position is full-time.

To be eligible for this role, you must have a bachelor's degree in Business Administration or a related field, and hands-on experience with CRM management, specifically HighLevel. Prior work experience in administration, sales, or marketing is a plus.

The ideal candidate will have the following responsibilities

	Core Skills	Secondary Skills
Must Have	<ul><li>Core Skill #1</li><li>Core Skill #2</li><li>Core Skill #3</li></ul>	<ul><li>Secondary Skill #1</li><li>Secondary Skill #2</li></ul>
Nice To Have	<ul><li>Core Skill #1</li><li>Core Skill #2</li></ul>	<ul><li>Secondary Skill #1</li></ul>

It is required that the candidate should be able to conduct market research to better understand the target audience. In this position, you will be responsible for the day-to-day operations and achieving results based on pre-set goals. Additionally, you will have to be proactive in managing the agency's demands.

Marketing Associate Qualifications and Skills

- Strong written and verbal communication skills.
- Excellent time management skills.
- A high level of attention to detail.

- Ability to work effectively within a team and independently.
- Ability to anticipate, understand and creatively solve problems or resolve issues.

Send your resumes to *Agency Email Address* along with an introduction video!

Pre-Screening Requirements

- Have at least a 15Mbps internet connection
- Send your DISC assessment along with your application
- Home setup has to be stress-tested:
    - Power backup in place
    - Home Office setup verified
    - Camera and lighting

Abilities:

- Able to work and communicate effectively with people.
- Able to work under pressure while adhering to even the shortest deadlines.
- Exceptional phone and video presence.
- Able to think on your feet.
- A proactive problem solver.
- Ability to learn new software tools fast.

Summary:

A hard-working, quality-driven Junior Executive. A well-rounded and open-minded professional marketing associate who eagerly listens and is committed to providing exceptional results. The ability to deliver targets and to build lasting relationships with our clients.

Example Two

About Our Company

RepStack is on a mission to innovate the hiring and working style. It helps agencies onboard the best virtual associates, handpicked according to the needs of our clients. They will handle accounts with smooth integration processes in minimal time.

Responsibilities

- Creating and planning a variety of PPC campaigns across a range of digital channels.
- Overseeing existing campaigns and making recommendations on how to optimize them.
- Analyzing trends and making data-driven decisions.
- Increasing sales and revenues of the agency through internet marketing.
- Producing detailed analyses and reports of campaigns.
- Presenting data and reports to a range of audiences.

Requirements

- Knowledge and hands-on experience of Google AdWords for local home services.
- Ability to think creatively and run campaigns on digital marketing platforms.
- Hands-on experience in running local service ads, Bing ads, and Facebook ads.
- Excellent written and verbal communication skills.
- Ability to communicate with prospects during video calls.
- Ability to present information effectively to a range of audiences.

As you can see in these two examples, there are noticeable differences. One is more detailed than the other. It gives you two options of whether you want it short and sweet or more detailed to weed out all the potential candidates.

While you're reviewing these two examples, think about which one best fits your agency. As you type your job description, make sure to include elements that best describe your agency. Finding a marketing associate who is already familiar with your niche is a huge timesaver.

Skills You Should Look Out For

A marketing associate must understand the content requirements for their client's online marketing efforts. They will work across all forms of social media and understand various marketing strategies at a high level while observing and understanding dynamic shifts in the paid advertising industry. You should look for the following skills:

- Launch Key Marketing Campaigns
    - Paid Ads
    - Cold Email Outreach
    - Lead Generation
- Social Media Management
    - Content Creation
    - Content Management
    - Social Media Outreach
    - Content Marketing
- Setting up & Managing your CRM
    - Automation & Workflows
    - Landing Pages & Forms
- Launch and Manage Podcasts/Webinars

CONTENT MARKETING

SOCIAL MEDIA

VIDEO EDITING

GRAPHIC DESIGN

MARKETING STRATEGY

Skills Explained

- **Content marketing.** Content marketing is a vital piece of the digital marketing puzzle, and you need a virtual assistant who understands the basics. They should be able to pitch in with managing a social media content calendar, help you with blog creation, understand the different content you can create, and be able to manage them all with an eye for detail.

- **Keyword research.** So much digital marketing these days comes down to your research keywords. A virtual assistant should understand the top keyword research tools and how to use them. This helps you find an audience that's looking for your service.

- **Social media management.** Social media is just as indispensable as any CRM tool you use. That's why it helps to have a virtual assistant who can help with lead generation via LinkedIn, Twitter, and more.

- **Strategy.** Can your virtual assistant handle the overarching strategy of your latest marketing campaigns? A marketing assistant can be more than a personal assistant here. They can be a member of the team that leverages their experience and expertise to optimize your campaigns.

- **Project management.** The project manager role often requires a specific talent for leadership and organization. But as you expand your team, there's no reason a virtual marketing associate can't help. They can organize marketing activities, help coordinate a remote team, and otherwise serve as the personal assistant to an entire marketing team.

- **Lead generation.** How do you bring in new leads to your business? Is too much time spent focusing on lead generation rather than doing great work for those clients you already have? A good virtual assistant can help generate leads through tasks such as selling by chatting on social media platforms and engaging in different groups using marketing strategies.

The Interview Process

As you gather a group of possible candidates, you will conduct interviews with each possible marketing associate. The interview is an important part of the hiring process, where you'll get the opportunity to really know the person you will potentially work with on a daily basis.

Phase 1 — Submitting a video resume

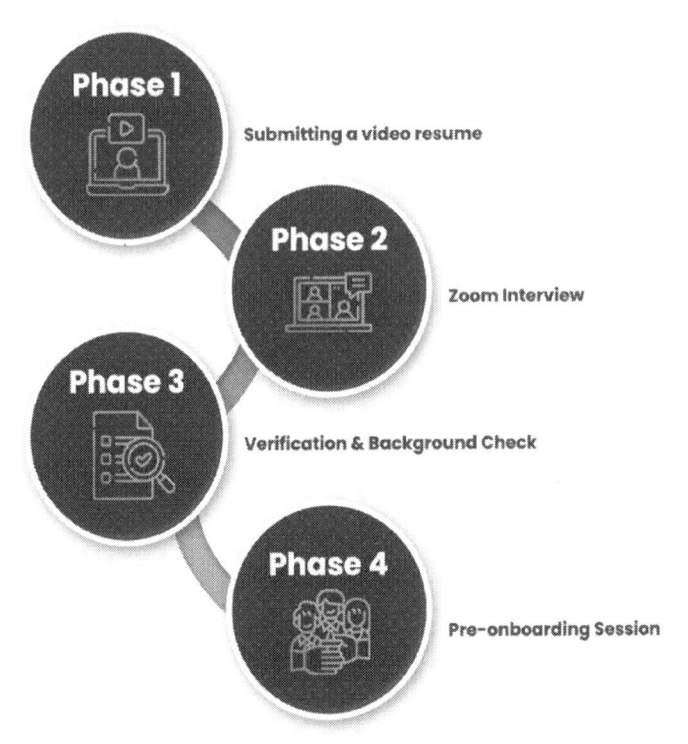

Phase 2 — Zoom Interview

Phase 3 — Verification & Background Check

Phase 4 — Pre-onboarding Session

Since you'll be hiring a virtual employee, it's important to be comfortable conducting a video call and that your potential employee is also comfortable doing that. After all, this will be the main mode of communication for the two of you, the other team members, and all potential clients.

During this interview, you'll get the opportunity to discover what the candidate is capable of and if they meet all the requirements for the job. To do this, you'll have to ask specific questions to get the type of responses you are looking for.

Here is a list of questions to get you started. As you review them, think about the type of questions you'd like to ask for the needs of your particular marketing associate.

- Tell me a little about yourself.

- Where are you from?
- What are your hobbies?
- What's important to you?
- What were you doing most recently? Why did you leave?
- What are your strengths?
- What do you feel you do best?
- What type of work have you done with others in the past?
- What does your work environment look like?
- Do you have a quiet, dedicated place to work?
- Do you have high-speed internet?

QUESTIONS TO ASK

TELL ME A LITTLE ABOUT YOURSELF?
WHAT TYPE OF WORK HAVE YOU DONE WITH OTHERS IN THE PAST?
WHAT INTERESTED YOU IN THIS POSITION?
WHAT ARE YOUR STRENGTHS?
WHAT DOES YOUR WORK ENVIRONMENT LOOK LIKE?

- What type of computer do you use?

- What interested you in this position?

- Are you looking for a short-term or long-term role?

- If we contacted your last employer and asked them to rate you on a scale from 1-10 (with 1 being terrible & 10 being the best), what would they rate you and why?

Communication Is Key

Communication is very important as you speak during an interview with a candidate. You'll want to make clear the responsibilities that you expect from your marketing associate, and how the two of you will engage in the future.

"

You'll want to make clear the responsibilities that you expect from your marketing associate, and how the two of you will engage in the future.

"

Below is a possible dialogue you can communicate with your candidate to ensure they can meet all your requirements.

1. **Responsiveness.** Be quick to reply when I send a message. This is an example of being on top of the ball. To me, that is the most important aspect of this role. If I send a message during work hours and don't hear back quickly, I will question how engaged you are in the position.

2. **Be resourceful.** I'll share with you what needs to be done and how to navigate my systems. But if you are stuck on something, try to solve it yourself before asking another team member or me. If it's something you could have solved by contacting support or doing a Google search first, then do that.

3. **Honesty.** Always be honest and forthcoming in all our dealings.

4. **Innovate.** We are an extremely fast-growing business. As you go about your job, we want you to find ways to improve your workflow. Make suggestions and enhance the way we operate by sharing ideas for possible improvement. This agency flourishes on teamwork.

5. **Work hard.** There is a lot to do. I'll need you by my side, proactively learning, innovating, and completing plenty of tasks each day.

6. **Ask for help.** Don't hesitate to ask if you need direction, resources, or support. I want you to be happy and fulfilled in your role. This should always be a win-win situation.

The above is a good way to communicate with your candidate to ensure they agree with your terms and expectations. You can use the above to customize your conversation as you clearly convey what you expect from your marketing associate. Remember to use your list of weaknesses during your interview and specify certain tasks you expect your potential marketing associate to complete.

> *Remember to use your list of weaknesses during your interview and specify certain tasks you expect your potential marketing associate to complete.*

Also, address what aspects of working together you deem are most important. Such as work ethic, honesty, or responsiveness.

Let your candidates know what you expect from them and what characteristics mean most to you. You don't just want a marketing associate who can just complete the work, but someone who can work well with your team members.

Remember that this marketing associate will need to be someone from whom you can expect a lot of potential in the future. They might start at entry-level, but many of our virtual associates eventually enter senior executive positions.

My first marking associate, Mashood, joined our team between the months of February and March 2021. He was originally supposed to sign on with another agency owner to be their marketing associate. But that agency owner decided to continue interviewing other candidates.

I feel that I was the lucky one in this situation because I was able to bring him into the team and get him right onto the daily tasks.

He took over the marketing department in a short amount of time as I gave him the vision of possible campaigns and social media management.

He's now running a six-person team at the tender age of 23. To this day, he's doing an amazing job and has turned the marketing department around single-handedly. Now he's the director of marketing for my agency.

That is what a virtual associate can do for any marketing agency.

Hiring Process Checklist

The graphic below shows the different stages you'll move through from beginning to end to give you a good idea of the overall process of hiring a marketing assistant. Use this as a good checklist to help you navigate the hiring process.

DEFINE A BUDGET
CREATE A JOB DESCRIPTION
START SHORTLISTING
FIND THE BEST
ASSESS THEIR ABILITIES
HIRE THE MARKETING ASSOCIATE
CREATE AND SIGN A CONTRACT

- <u>Define a budget</u>: Decide how much you can afford hourly and yearly for a marketing associate. Keep in mind that many freelancers are business owners; they pay their own taxes, insurance, and overhead. So, their hourly rates may be slightly higher than an employee's. A USA-based associate usually starts at $20/ hour. An offshore quality associate will be between $11 and $18/ hour.

- <u>Create a job description</u>: Be extremely clear on your job description so you can attract the right people. Use the samples at the beginning of the chapter to help you get started.

- <u>Start shortlisting</u>: After you post your job description, it is time to start shortlisting candidates for your business. This process can be time-consuming, so make sure to pace yourself.

- <u>Find the best</u>: Start interviewing your shortlisted candidates by setting up a time and date and then scheduling a video call meeting.

- <u>Assess their abilities</u>: Conduct an interview. Most freelancers work remotely, so this may be the only time you'll ever "meet" the person. When you conduct a video interview, you can gain a better sense of the person's abilities and fit than just talking to them over the phone. I also recommend a Slack-based interview so you can check their written communications.

- <u>Hire the marketing associate</u>: When discussing project details, understand that both of you are negotiating an agreement that covers when the person can start, what they'll deliver, when those deliverables are expected, and payment terms.

- <u>Create and sign a contract</u>: Make your agreement official with a contract. Good contracts are detailed yet concise, so they're very clear. With platforms like Upwork and Fiverr, this aspect is built-in. If you're hiring locally, you should have a version of a contract, making sure both parties sign them, and they are reported properly to your accounting department and the IRS. And, with a company like RepStack, we take care of the contracts on both sides.

Onboarding Your New Marketing Associate

Once you've chosen your ideal candidate for your marketing associate, it's now time to start the onboarding process. Though they will join your team already possessing many skills, there are key details about your agency that they will need to know.

For example, your marketing associate needs to know your message. When they understand your agency's purpose, niche, and brand, they are able to create material that matches those ideals.

> *Your marketing associate needs to know your message. When they understand your agency's purpose, niche, and brand, they are able to create material that matches those ideals.*

Use the following checklist to determine what your onboarding process is going to look like for your marketing associate. Remember that you want to set them up for success instead of letting them figure it all out on their own.

- What tools need to be set up for them? Who will set those up? Create a checklist.
- What will their orientation process look like?
  - Initial Day
  - Accessing Tools / Software
  - Communication Expectations
- How will they be trained in what you expect them to do?
  - Orientation on the roll
  - Training on the day-to-day
- What will they be expected to report daily / weekly / monthly?

- How will you gauge their performance?
- Communicate the expectations from day one.

As you create your onboarding process for a new marketing associate, keep in mind that you can delegate this process to one of your managers to oversee. It's good to ensure that your newest team member has all the tools they need to be successful. But you don't need to oversee their onboarding process.

Instead, after you create your onboarding checklist, delegate it to your marketing director to ensure that it is completed. It is better for the marketing associate to learn from their direct supervisor to start building those key relationships. Then you can expect a report back on how the onboarding process is going instead of having to manage the entire program.

Management, Accountability, and Ongoing Training

When your new marketing associate has been successfully hired and onboarded, then it's important to have a plan for their management, accountability, and ongoing training. If your agency currently has a marketing team, then the person who will be managing the new marketing associate will be your marketing director.

However, if you don't have a marketing team or director, then you'll be the one managing your new employee. You have to decide how often the new marketing associate will be checking in with you or the marketing director.

When will the new hire meet with you for feedback? Do you want to schedule weekly or monthly check-ins? Make that decision now so you can best give your marketing associate clear expectations and the type of communication you prefer.

In order to successfully manage your marketing associate, you'll have to give them certain measurements to meet and tools to use in order to be accountable for their work. You can have them use a program like Time Doctor so that they can track the hours they are working while also offering screenshots every few minutes to prove they are doing the work.

> *To successfully manage your marketing associate, you'll have to give them certain measurements to meet and tools to use in order to be accountable for their work.*

In addition, you can have them send you an end-of-day report of all the tasks they completed to compare it with the results. At any time, you should be able to check in on your marketing associate and verify the work they are completing each day.

Certain measurements that your marketing associate will be working on during the meeting are based on the number of campaigns they are overseeing for either your agency or your client. Then you can watch as those numbers start to grow and see how well the marketing associate is able to multitask and handle the pressure of a full workload.

This new employee is going to grow as your agency grows. Therefore, you want to ensure they have all the training they need now and right onto the day they will be in a senior position. Successful business owners always invest in their employees. Ensure that you do the same for your marketing associate.

Here is the 90-day plan I give all of my marketing associates so they can focus on improving their skills. It includes several different types of training that can strengthen their skillset and, in turn, improve my agency.

90 Day RepStack Success Academy Learning Path

	Month 1 (Day 1-30)	Month 2 (Day 30-60)	Month 3 (Day 60-90)
Week 1	o Fundamentals of Digital Marketing o HighLevel and CRM Masterclass o Email Deliverability & Email Builders	o Social Media Marketing Certification o Google Analytics, GA4 o Google Tag Manager	o SEO Training Certifications o SEO Advance Level Training o On Page and Off Page SEO
Week 2	o Cold Outreach o Cold Email Marketing o MailChimp o Active Campaign	o Facebook Business Manager o Facebook Ads Manager o Social Media Marketing Mastery	o Data and Extensive Keyword Research o SEMrush, Ahrefs

			○ WordPress Website Development
Week 3	○ Automations and Triggers ○ Dream 100 ○ Hillsberg Method ○ Chat Bot Integration ○ CRM Workflows	○ Facebook Meta Certifications ○ Google Search Ads ○ Google Display Network ○ Google Ads Training	○ WordPress Training ○ Facebook Ad Creatives ○ Dollar A Day ○ Content Syndication
Week 4	○ Basic Keyword Research ○ Content Marketing ○ Marketing Copy	○ GMB Certification ○ LinkedIn Ads ○ TikTok Ads Mastery ○ YouTube Ads	○ Content Marketing ○ Podcasts and Webinars ○ Video Editing and Graphic Design

Working with a new marketing associate can leave you a bit anxious. After all, you want to see the results right away. But it's realistic to expect big results within the first 90 days versus within the first month.

Many RepStack employees have been able to give the agency owners they are paired with amazing results because of the intense hiring process I implement as well as the continued education I require my associates to complete within their first 90 days.

As you follow the same process I implement, you'll be happily surprised at the results you'll soon discover with your own marketing associate. By first hiring a marketing associate and working with them for some 90 days, you'll pave the way for hiring the next key roles for your agency.

134

Bonus tip: <u>To help streamline this process, hire a marketing agency coach who has blueprints for rolling out some of the initial duties of your marketing associate.</u> This will shorten the learning curve and allow you to bring in people that will get them to follow the growth track immediately. You can also partner with a company like RepStack, which has a roadmap that is ready to go so your new associate can run with it from day one. In addition, roll out a bonus structure from day one to give your new employees incentive and help keep them engaged with their job from month to month.

Chapter 6:

The Marketing Associate Case Studies

Working with a marketing associate will show you a world of possibilities while also opening the doors to new opportunities for your agency. You'll soon learn that a marketing associate is an integral part of your agency and therefore needs to be taken seriously.

This team member will dedicate a full-time schedule to creating internal marketing campaigns for your agency. In return, they'll need frequent feedback in order to set them up for success.

That is why continued training and routine check-ins are important for a new marketing associate. These are tasks that are done during the first 90 days in order to set them and your agency up for long-term success.

Throughout this chapter, you'll be able to see this model of hiring and training a marketing associate come to life through genuine experiences. These case studies not only highlight the desired growth for the agency but how these marketing associates are then promoted into senior positions.

Remember that a marketing associate is going to be with your agency long-term. Their potential is endless. Just like the new opportunities, you'll get to experience one on your team. Take my word for it and the words of the agency owners you'll get to read about next.

Rudy Hettrick, Owner of Floor Coating Marketers, and Remsha, Digital Marketing Associate

REPSTACK CASE STUDY

WORKING WITH UME LAILA HAS BEEN FANTASTIC. LAILA IS JUST AMAZING

RUDY HETTRICK | REMSHA

One of the most amazing testimonials I've ever heard concerning working with a new marketing associate comes from Rudy Hettrick, owner of Floor Coating Marketers. Rudy's years of experience in the construction industry make his agency so unique.

When Rudy moved away from the construction world, he wanted to solve problems for many of the floor coating companies today. He created his agency to help bring in more customers for these companies. He solved problems for websites and advertising without needing to be on Angie's List or Yelp.

Rudy and I are both a part of the same mastermind group, the 7 Figure Agency conducted by Josh Nelson. Being both from Canada, we connected right away. It was great to hear his story of starting a digital marketing agency after years of experience working for other companies and focusing a lot of his time on sales.

When asked why he started his digital marketing agency, he explained, "Why not?" I love this response because it relates to, "If not me, then who?" Creating a digital marketing agency made sense for Rudy as it fits perfectly with his personality. Having a passion for developing technology and game development, he then transferred that passion and skill set into creating websites.

The bottom line, you have to love what you do. Even on mornings that are hard to get going, getting to work, for Rudy, is like being paid to play video games because he has so much passion for his work. Now he is a successful digital marketing specialist who has helped many floor coating businesses thrive. He will do exactly what he promises his clients.

One of the key success elements for Rudy was hiring two virtual marketing assistants from RepStack who helped him manage his day-to-day tasks. He hired an Account Manager for his digital marketing agency to match his unique process of working with clients. In addition, he has a Sales Development Rep that can follow Rudy's core beliefs and work ethic to attract new clients.

But what Rudy discovered, as all agency owners find out, is that once you solve problems for clients, you have to also solve your own problems. That is why he is dedicated to hiring Remsha as a digital marketing associate.

In a recent interview, Rudy stated that "RepStack is an amazing agency for agency owners. They have all their ducks in a row. All the things that we would normally have to train for, RepStack takes care of that."

> *RepStack is an amazing agency for agency owners. They have all their ducks in a row. All the things that we would normally have to train for, RepStack takes care of that.*

"They bring on only candidates who are qualified and seem to have a really high skill set. Our new marketing associate, Remsha, clearly showed how much she wanted to learn about my agency and grow with it. I really appreciate the type of effort that she puts into her work."

"I highly recommend using RepStack for any virtual associate that you might need. It takes so much workload off of your plate to know that you're working with a qualified marketing associate before you even get started. All of the training is completed and the associate is able to join the team easily."

"Plus, their customer service is outstanding. If I were to have any issues, I know it would be a quick turnaround to my inquiry. They are very easy to work with, and always so kind. If you are on the fence of working with a marketing associate, you don't need to be. They are a game-changer. It's a pleasure to work with them, so take the plunge."

> *If you are on the fence of working with a marketing associate, you don't need to be. They are a game-changer. It's a pleasure to work with them, so take the plunge.*

From Rudy's testimonial, it's clear to see how happy he is with a marketing associate. He's been working with Remsha for close to a year now and has seen amazing results for his agency.

When talking with Remsha and her experience working at Rudy's agency, she gave me a detailed explanation of the work that she does each day for the agency. It's clear to see why she is such a great match for Floor Coating Marketers.

"I am a digital marketing associate where I get to work with Rudy and his team. To give you a sneak peek into my day, I usually start by check-in on Woodpecker. There are currently two campaigns going on, and every day I will check to see what contact information has come in through those campaigns."

"With the new emails of potential clients, I update the Excel file that is shared with the sales department to give them new leads to contact for a discovery call. In a way, I am also working alongside the sales development reps."

"I also create social media posts using Canva. I'll create images that are then scheduled to be posted on Rudy's social media platforms. I normally create the images a month in advance to go right alongside the marketing campaigns that are being planned out."

"To do this, I create social media calendars with the dates each image or video will be posted, along with the text and hashtags that will go with the digital content. Using SocialPilot, I'm able to schedule all of these posts in advance and select which platforms they will post to."

"I will also schedule blog posts and other content to appear on the business platforms using LocalViking. I've found that these websites are really easy to use and initially learn. Now I'm managing tasks that my supervisors originally had to handle. I enjoy being able to take on this workload and create results for Rudy and his team."

"In addition, I also manage our Dream 100 Outreach Tracker for the year. Every day I am prospecting all the social media platforms, the blog, and the emails to make connections with new clients and book discovery calls for the sales department."

"When I complete all my tasks, I will send Rudy an end-of-the-day report through email. That way Rudy can always see what I am tackling every day and the progress I am able to make."

After talking with Remsha, it is clear to see how much she enjoys the tasks that she gets to complete with Rudy each day. She is focused on the message that Rudy is trying to convey with his agency and brand. In return, she is able to create bright and engaging images and videos that can be found on social media.

All of Remsha's activities are geared toward generating new leads for the sales department. This is the job of the marketing associate. They are involved in many things throughout their day, but the culmination of all those things is more leads for the sales department, which, in turn, means growth.

Remsha's goal in working for Floor Coating Marketers is to eventually become the director of marketing through her experience with the company. She takes pride in the work she completes each day and enjoys seeing improved engagement on all the social media platforms because of the content she creates.

April Edwards, Owner of AE Design Co., and Hamza, Digital Marketing Associate

REPSTACK CASE STUDY

THE POINT IS THAT HE'S VERY COMMITTED, A GREAT PART OF THE TEAM, AND WE ALL ENJOY WORKING WITH HIM.

APRIL EDWARDS | HAMZA ALI

"I've seen many other agencies fail to provide intimate and tailored, forward-thinking results that small businesses need." This is one of the first things April Edwards told our client success manager as we talked about her recent experience. She shared her passion for being a marketing agency owner and why she started AE Design Co.

"After years of working with other marketing agencies, I was never quite satisfied with the results that these big companies delivered. Something always seemed to be lacking. Maybe you've worked with a freelancer, a friend, or tried to do the marketing yourself?"

"Many times, these scenarios lead to wasted time and frustration. The do-it-yourself approach, just like with construction, doesn't work well in marketing either. AE Design Co. has had to come in many times to clean things up and get our busy clients back on track."

"

Marketing takes the know-how to do it right.

"

"Marketing takes the know-how to do it right. So, in 2012, I left the big marketers and founded AE Design Co. Working one-on-one with small clients meant I could give them the personal attention they deserved. I could sit down with each client and discuss their big dreams and goals and the marketing obstacles standing in their way. I could provide tailored advice instead of using the same checklist for everyone. And I could provide a better return on their investment."

When our client success manager asked her what she was most proud of, she said, "Truly educating my clients on what all this "marketing stuff" means first! Only then could they more confidently make informed decisions to grow their business with a consistent flow of high-quality leads and better customers."

"As our clients grew, we did too! We had to! So, I expanded our team to keep providing personal, tailored plans to each of our clients. Today, I get to work every day with this amazing team of strategists, marketers, designers & developers."

One of the new team members that April added to her team was Hamza, a digital marketing associate. As her small agency grew, she needed associates who would work just as hard as she was and who also possessed the ability to grow.

When our client success manager asked her about the last few months with Hamza, she explained, "Hamza was the ideal person for me. He's ambitious and in general, a pleasure to work with. I was actually seeing him stay up later than I was working, so I had to let him know that it was alright for him to change his hours. The point is that he's very committed, a great part of the team, and we all enjoy working with him."

> *The point is that he's very committed, a great part of the team, and we all enjoy working with him.*

It was great talking with April about the changes she's seen in her agency since bringing Hamza onto the team. While talking with Hamza himself, he shared with our client success manager the tasks he normally completes by the end of each day. It shows how committed he is to the agency and his dedication to his work.

"I begin each day by logging onto our Team Works website, where I can see the list of tasks and projects I've been assigned. I'm able to see the rating of each task to understand their priorities, as well as their descriptions."

"With these lists of tasks, I decide which ones to tackle first by their order of priority. I keep close contact with April through Slack to ensure I haven't missed any important tasks that perhaps haven't made it onto the list. I've found that this frequent communication keeps me focused on the most important tasks she has for me, but also reassures her that I'm going to complete them right away."

"Outside of that, I also work with AE Design Co.'s clients to create funnels, campaigns, and email marketing. I will build new templates for these clients, or sometimes refresh an old template to fit the client's needs."

"In addition, I use Woodpecker to manage the agency's marketing campaigns. I'll use that to gather the contact information for new prospects and make sure that the new list is sent to the sales department to book discovery calls."

"One of the things I also love to do is creating content for social media platforms with Canva. I can load all the content I create into the online dashboard so it can be distributed to the different social media platforms."

"Sometimes, I will also edit articles or create reports that will be used for April's blog, including adding digital content. This often includes the videos that April will record, which I will then edit and put either on her social media or blog.

"What I love about working for April is getting to see how the content I am creating is bringing in more clients for the agency. I think what April has created is pretty amazing after her years of experience in this industry, and I truly enjoy working with her and her team to help new clients each day."

This is a powerful testimony of a marketing associate going above and beyond when they enjoy what they do each day and believe in the agency's mission. That is why training a new marketing associate is vital so they can learn more about the agency's purpose and how they now fit into the model of that purpose.

Jennifer Crego, Owner of Type B Studio and Salman, Digital Marketing Associate

REPSTACK CASE STUDY

HE SHOWED HOW SKILLED HE TRULY WAS, AND HOW DEDICATED HE BECAME TO MY MISSION WITH THE AGENCY

JENNIFER CREGO | SALMAN AHMAD

I enjoyed talking with Jennifer Crego because she is the owner of a small digital marketing agency. She caters to a small niche of clients and is very successful in what she does. Having spoken with countless agency owners over the years, I've met owners of large companies and small businesses. Since Jennifer is a small business owner, she is able to solve issues for other business owners. During her conversation with our client success manager, she said, "Before starting Type B Studio, I spent over a decade as the Director of Business Development for an online retailer. There is no industry more focused on online conversions than e-commerce."

"I founded Type B Studio in 2014 and I, alongside a small team of experts, now focus our collective experience on building effective websites for small businesses to help get them seen online."

"Our websites are designed for conversion. There are a ton of small business websites that are designed to simply look good. I believe that a website that doesn't convert website visitors and truly help the business succeed is a waste of money and effort."

"I don't do jargon, and I don't believe in overcomplicating things. I'm a friendly small business owner who likes to get to know other small business owners."

Jennifer is an expert at finding solutions for small business owners, especially when it comes to website design. But while she excelled in her niche, she struggled with getting her name in front of new clients.

That's when she decided to bring Salman onto her team, someone who specializes in the marketing techniques that she was more focused on for her niche. With Salman on the team, she was able to hit all the new marketing goals for her agency.

"I will admit that management hasn't always been my strong suit. But getting to work with Salman, who was already trained in the marketing techniques I was looking for, made it easy. I didn't have to worry about if he was going to complete tasks the way that I would. Instead, he showed how skilled he truly was, and how dedicated he became to my mission with the agency."

A few months after Jennifer and Salman started working together, our client success manager touched base with Salman to hear how he was doing. Not only was he enjoying working with Type B Studio, but he was getting to use all his strengths to create results for the agency.

He described his daily activities as follows: "At the beginning of the day, I sign into Time Doctor so I can track my hours and detail which tasks I am working on at the time. I like to show Jennifer what I am working on throughout the day, and this software lets me do that." "After that, I'll log onto Slack and wish everyone a good morning. Next, I'll sign into Team Work to review my tasks for the day. It's also nice to see the work that my team is doing, which just comprises of me, Jen, and Georgia. It provides a friendly and team working environment."

"Today I worked on creating engaging social media profiles for Type B Studio clients. But first I have to fix their logo to be more engaging and to fit into the requirements of each social media platform."

"I will also check the agency's emails to ensure the clients are happy with the digital products they are receiving, and address any concerns. For example, one of the clients wanted an updated logo, so I went ahead and took care of that for them right away. Their original logo was very pixelated, so I was able to recreate it so it had a much higher resolution."

"Some of my time is taken up by researching and writing. Right now, I'm working on a landing page for a client who is a life coach. I get to collaborate with her on creating a great landing page and funnel for her potential clients."

"I'm also creating a checklist for another client that required a bit of research. It's a copywriting checklist that targets prospective clients and convinces them to move forward with the client's solutions to their problems. While doing so, I was able to discover what kind of marketing solutions the client actually desires based on the services they offer their own customers."

Salman is an ingenious marketing associate because he's able to predict the needs of his clients and upsell them. Not only has this brought the team recurring clients, but Jennifer is able to offer a wider variety of services she wouldn't have been able to do without Salman's help. He's a perfect fit for their small team of hard workers and go-getters.

Joe & Dominique, Owners of Beyond Creative Digital Growth Agency, and Hajra, Digital Marketing Specialist

REPSTACK CASE STUDY

THE RELATIONSHIP BETWEEN US AND THE REST OF THE TEAM HAS BEEN WORKING OUT VERY WELL. WE'RE HAPPY TO HAVE HAJRA AS PART OF OUR TEAM OF MARKETING ASSOCIATES

JOE & DOMINIQUE | HAJRA JAFRI

Owners of Beyond Creative, an agency started in 2011 and based out of Fort Lauderdale, Joe and Dominique took their combined experience as marketing directors for other companies and decided to create their own agency.

Their niche is power sport, marine, and RV dealerships to help them generate and manage internal leads so they can "Sell More Fun." Their campaigns have been so successful that they have been seen on NBC, FOX, CBS, and ABC. With their sudden growth and spotlight, they needed to expand their team.

Therefore, they hired Hajra to be their digital marketing associate. She's been on their team for a short while, but they already have great things to say about her progress in their agency.

"So far, so good," Dominique started during a conversation between the three of us. "I can't think of one negative thing to say in the short time she's been on the team. She's great, a very smart woman, and a wonderful multitasker. I'm surprised every day that we're able to throw almost any task her way, and she's able to roll with it right away without any surprise."

> *I'm surprised every day that we're able to throw almost any task her way, and she's able to roll with it right away without any surprise.*

"She is very thorough as well, which has been a true blessing. She's catching on very quickly, and she already has important tasks that are just hers to manage. She'll always ask the right questions when she needs to, but for the most part, she is self-sufficient."

"The relationship between us and the rest of the team has been working out very well. We're happy to have Hajra as part of our team of marketing associates."

After getting to speak to Joe and Dominique about the sudden growth in their agency, they made it clear how fundamental it is to have a marketing associate not only take care of the agency's needs but also the needs of all their new clients. All the work that they used to manage on their own, they are now able to hand to their new associate.

While talking with Hajra about her short time with this new agency, she had nothing but pleasant things to say. She felt well suited for the position and absorbed all the new training she was given when she accepted the position.

She was able to finish the training quickly and learn more details about the agency's target audience. By doing so, she was then able to provide unique solutions for not only the agency but the clients as well.

"A normal day for me begins with checking my emails and talking with the clients that I have been assigned to create digital marketing content for. I'll review any new tasks for the day or any pending assignments from the client or from Joe and Dominique."

"As the main marketing specialist for this agency, I take care of a lot of different tasks which can include coordinating with the designer, creating and implementing different marketing strategies for our clients, and pulling reports to review analytics."

"I get to use a variety of different tools each day such as Dash Clicks, Spy Fu, Agency Analytics, and Google Ads. I often have several Excel documents open at one time to upload content for social media or brainstorm different ideas for possible campaigns."

"I enjoy creating fresh ideas and then seeing them come alive. Even though the digital marketing industry is not new, there are new ways to capture a viewer's attention. I like creating those new ideas and seeing them be a big success for the agency."

"Some of my ideas come from reviewing previous ads in the Facebook Ad Library. I can often get some really good ideas either for the agency or to solve a problem for a current client. I like to learn what has already been done and then improve upon it."

"I like working with others on my team, such as the graphic designer to create the images and video content for various campaigns. I have the freedom to give details on the content I want to see created before I'm able to implement it, creating a good working relationship that also gives the graphic designer plenty of creative tasks to complete each day."

"Sometimes I'll go into Photoshop myself to create different graphics to be a good team player and ensure the workload is shared."

"I'll also work in the CRM to create different landing pages and funnels for either the agency or our current clients. I'll also put mechanics in place for all upcoming webinars to get those registered and capture all the viewer's contact information for discovery calls afterward."

"Even though it's often a busy day here with the agency, I'm really loving it. I can't wait to see what the future holds."

The fact that Hajra has been with this agency for only a short time is a testimonial to the growth a marketing associate can offer any agency. She is now in a senior position with high hopes of further growth she can attain and what she can offer to the agency in return.

Each one of these case studies showcased how a marketing associate is an integral part of the agencies they work for. They are someone who can be easily trained and must be taken seriously. When you give the care needed to your marketing associate, they will flourish on their own.

These full-time team members will need constant feedback in the beginning in order to set them up for success. But most new marketing associates are able to rise up the ladder in their teams in less than a year.

I've seen this happen in both of my companies. With my digital marketing agency, I've come to understand how important it is to set up this key role before the others can be established. In the next chapter, you'll see how a sales development rep can add even more growth, but that only happens after 3-6 months when clear campaigns are established by a marketing associate. With clear campaigns in place, a sales development representative can achieve success.

Chapter 7:

Secret 2: The Sales Development Rep

Once you have finished laying the first brick of the marketing department, the next brick to the foundation of your agency is for the sales department. You do this by placing a sales development rep (sales associate, sales assistant, appointment setter) on your team.

By placing the right person in this role, the marketing funnels created by your sales associate can now be acted upon. The sales development rep can work from a six-point funnel and begin contacting the prospective client by email or phone call. The conversation with a new client is unlocked.

The rebuilt system created by the marketing associate allows the sales development rep to respond to all sorts of communication outlets, from social media messages to emails and even pre-recorded voicemails. While you may think having a marketing associate is the solution to all your time management problems, what you're about to discover in this chapter is the second secret to unlocking growth for your agency.

A sales development rep ensures a high return on investment for each marketing campaign.

Once your marketing associate is in place and generating more leads for your agency, you don't want to load yourself down with countless clients to email and call. Instead, you can rely on a sales development rep, commonly known as an appointment setter, to take on these tasks.

Remember the case study in chapter two with John Nelson and Henry? Henry was able to close almost 92 deals within the first three months of working for John Nelson's agency. He was dedicated to the agency's mission and had a great personality that clients loved. He could easily talk to prospective clients, identify their needs, and close many deals. Like a marketing associate, a sales development rep can take on a long list of responsibilities. By having a sales development rep on your team, you'll find your agency becoming more automated as the basic mechanics are put into place.

Now that you have marketing funnels and leads in place with your marketing associate, 3-6 months afterward, you can expect to bring on a sales development rep to your team to start contacting the new list of prospective clients.

As you grow your agency and scale it, hiring becomes the most important thing you can do. This is because you've run out of your own personal ability to meet with everyone, talk to everyone, and make sure every client is happy.

Hiring becomes way more important than it was before to get essential individuals on your teams. You might be doing everything for your agency now; you spend time ensuring all your clients are on board, and you address your clients' concerns every day. However, you need to ensure that you project the future of your agency and envisage it turning out into a larger organization.

Position Overview

A sales development representative (SDR) is responsible for proactively setting sales appointments for the director of business development. This is done by following up with inbound leads & reaching out to your prospect list by calling, emailing, texting & social messaging.

Sales development reps assist the sales team by outreaching prospective clients and scheduling discovery and strategy calls. In today's modern age, a sales development rep has to be a ten-in-one soldier with expertise in digital outreach, psychology, and analytical skills.

The sales development rep can focus on inbound and outbound sales by utilizing the marketing campaigns and funnels established by the marketing department. An SDR takes the time to contact clients who may have been no-shows for appointments or follow up with clients who download the free lead magnet. Additionally, sales development reps provide full customer and administrative support. They will book discovery calls and manage schedules.

You can expect your sales development rep to:

- "Clean up" your prospect list
- Answer and direct 70-80 phone calls a day
- Manage communication and answer emails
- Prepare and organize databases and reports
- Manage social media accounts and replies

- Handles customer and employer information confidentially

- Take notes or transcribe meetings conducted online and share minutes of meetings.

- Schedule meetings, manage calendar and appointments

- Create purchase orders and track and manage payments

- Manage filing systems, update records, and organize documentation

- Online research for materials and sources for presentations

- All calls are recommended to be started via your CRMs (HighLevel, HubSpot, etc.), so there is an accurate log of activity & calls are recorded.

- Each call/message should have an outcome noted in your CRM.

- Scheduled appointments will be set using your calendar link (your sales assistant can set that up for you).

Eventually, you'll be able to rely on your SDR to make discovery calls and book strategy sessions in order to close the deal on their own.

> *Eventually, you'll be able to rely on your SDR to make discovery calls and book strategy sessions in order to close the deal on their own.*

As you read over the list a few times, start to think how much free time you'd have on your hands if you had a sales development rep who would take care of these tasks for you. The major goal of working with these three key roles is to allow you the freedom to focus on what you deem important.

Working with a sales development rep to take care of these tasks for you allows your agency to move further into growth mode. By following this tactic of hiring a sales development rep 90 days after a marketing associate, you're moving closer to reaching that 1-million-dollar mark within 2-3 years.

While you have a clear idea of what a sales development rep can do for you, the benchmarks you can expect from this employee include the following:

- → Calls / Connections (Cold & Warm calls, emails, and social media)
    - ◆ 80+ per day (*as long as you have a solid prospect list, marketing funnels built out by the sales team, and CRM systems*)

- 400 per week
- 1600 per month

→ Strategy Call Appointments Booked
- 3-4 per week
- 15 per month

Something you can do now is write down the number of connections and calls you are able to make each day. This can include calling prospective clients once you have their contact information from your key campaigns and funnels.

Are you currently calling or connecting with 80 prospective clients a day?

Can you imagine the growth for your agency if you could?

Though we all know that calling 80 prospective clients a day doesn't mean you're going to have 80 new clients purchasing services from you. Instead, from that 80, you can expect to have strategy sessions with 4 of them a week to land solid deals. But imagine the time you'd have on your hands if you could hire one employee to take care of all those calls and connections each day. All you'd have to worry about is meeting with those four interested clients each week to have amazing strategy meetings.

Just like a marketing associate, sales development reps will also create end-of-day reports that you'll receive in order to track their progress. Sample end-of-day reports that you could expect from an SDR include the following:

Sample 1

Hey Rudy,

Here's what I've been up to:

- Made a check-in call with a potential lead we obtained from Facebook. (Lead called back)
- Had a meeting with the client to discuss the goals and new scripts.
- Reviewed the new sales script you sent me.
- Made 23 video request calls.
    - 11 received
    - 8 voicemails
    - 3 not received
    - 1 move forward conversation (video request accepted).
- Made 20 follow-up calls.
    - 12 received
    - 6 voicemails
    - 2 not received
- Followed 8 contacts on Facebook.

Sample 2

Hey Josh,

This is what I was up to today.

Updated Discovery Call Tracker Sheets

Researched for Dream 100 Prospects

Updated Dream 100 Prospects Data Sheet

Updated Discovery Calls Scheduled sheet

1. Dream 100 Calls made: 5

    New Leads Confirmation Calls: 2

    - Connected: 0
    - Strategy Calls Confirmed: 0
    - Scheduled Call Back: 0
    - No Answer/Answering Machines: 2
    - Wrong/Invalid Numbers: 0

2. 2021 Checklist Download Calls: 23

    - Connected: 2
    - Scheduled Call Back: 2
    - No Answer/Voicemail: 13
    - Wrong/Invalid Numbers: 5
    - Discovery Calls Booked: 0
    - Strategy Calls Booked: 0
    - Follow-up calls: 3

3. No Answer Follow-up Calls: 26

- Connected: 1
- Discovery Calls Booked: 0
- Strategy Calls Booked: 0
- Scheduled Call Back: 1
- No Answer/Voicemail: 24
- Wrong/Invalid Numbers: 1
- Self-Gen Prospect Calls: 0
- Hot leads Went Cold Calls: 0

Will see you guys tomorrow
Thanks!

Not only did these SDRs make close to 80 calls a day, but they were also working on other research projects. They had additional tasks outside those phone classes to help in other areas of the department.

Can you imagine receiving a report like that every day? This helps you to see how having a sales development rep can lead your agency towards an automotive process instead of a company that you have to constantly micromanage.

This is a topic that is really near and dear to my heart because agency owners are great at so many things. But it's hard to be good at everything every day. Eventually, you'll be completely burnt out.

The Benefits of Working with a Sales Development Rep

Hiring your first sales development rep is laying the first brick in setting up your agency's sales department. Eventually, you'll add to this team, and your first SDR will become a sales manager. That is what the future of your sales department looks like.

A sales development rep has the ability to perform several tasks, as mentioned above. But beyond this associate taking on tasks that you no longer have to worry about, they offer a wide range of benefits for your agency. Some of the benefits of a sales development rep are as follows:

1. Save time and money

Sales development representatives (SDRs) free up a lot of time for you to exert more effort in attending strategy calls and making strategies to support your agency.

2. Expanding the sales force

"

Sales development reps are not just appointment setters. They are an extension of your sales team.

"

Sales development reps are not just appointment setters. They are an extension of your sales team. He or she can develop a customized script that focuses on your products and services. They can also carry out this task by gathering information regarding what sort of businesses should be contacted and who the key decision-makers are.

3. Cost-effective solution

Working with a remote sales development rep — whether locally or overseas — is indeed a cost-effective solution. They can manage their own virtual schedule (just like an appointment setter), so you don't have to worry and manage additional staff. You'll get end-of-the-day reports and don't have to worry about micromanaging an SDR.

- Update daily agenda on CRM.
- Follow up and send reminders to prospects who have booked a strategy session
- Follow up with leads generated from inbound marketing
    START OFF BY DIALING THE INBOUND AND OUTBOUND CALLS OF THE DAY
- Dial virtual hiring guide opt-ins
- No show on discovery call leads
- Dial partially qualified leads
- Dial chase-up leads

4. A new breed of sales developers

With thousands of competitors on the market, marketing yourself and your agency and getting noticed is no simple task.

Cold calling is the old way of making sales. These SDRs are committed to their agencies because they want to have a career. They have even gained more experience and knowledge than regular appointment setters because of the diversity of client base they handle. Their goal is to become a sales executive with their MBA in digital marketing.

They can reach out to clients wherever possible — on social media, by text messages, and by email. This is the type of person who is going to be representing your business now.

This gives an agency owner the free time to assess the overall sales approach of his agency and determine what needs to be changed for it to be more effective.

5. Generating and nurturing leads

There are various phases in a prospect's journey, each with its own set of challenges. Having an effective nurturing system in place can make it much easier to nurture leads and turn them into clients.

A sales development rep can create a list of warm and cold leads (top/bottom of the sales funnel) and book them on the sales manager's calendar when ready.

> *Lead nurturing can lead to a 20% increase in sales opportunities*

Important reminder: If you don't have the resources to run full-funnel marketing, remember you need a marketing associate first who can generate some highly qualified leads to jumpstart your growth mode. You will not see the benefits of an SDR until these mechanics are in place.

6. Data and analysis

A lead list must be created to reach the most interested prospects. Setting up a discovery call that will result in a closed transaction is more likely to succeed if you have a qualified list.

To do this, a sales development rep can gather and analyze the relevant data to determine the right people who are responsive to an agency's product or service, as well as those who are the appropriate decision-makers.

7. Dedicated skills

Statistically, sales development reps excel because they are great communicators, fast learners, and they understand the complexity of products, services, and solutions within an agency. They are fast on their toes and not afraid to put in the hard work.

8. Avoid what you dislike

If you're like me, there's no doubt that it's time to hire an associate rather than lose a sales opportunity. Avoid the tasks you don't like to do by relying on a team member to tackle them instead. That is why a sales development rep is an important part of your team.

9. Perform other tasks on the side

A sales development rep can also be invaluable in surveying your customer base, introducing new solutions, running a database reactivation campaign, etc.

10. Easy to track

Appointment scheduling services provide a trackable and much-improved ROI over traditional sales approaches. It will be easy to see what your sales development rep is accomplishing every day.

11. Taking it a notch-higher

The most popular approach for marketing is to move prospecting and appointment scheduling from selling. One in four businesses, or 25%, are adopting the new paradigm of separating prospecting and appointment setting from selling.

More often than not, digital marketing agencies rely on their SDRs to book appointments and close deals. They can maximize the number of appointments booked by their high level of scripts. This is a new-age way of selling where the SDR works very closely with the marketing department.

That is why establishing these three key roles leads to growth for your agency.

Having The Mechanics In Place

Before validating potential leads, sales development reps answer inbound calls (from current clients or customers) from the agency's perspective. After the sales development reps' successful validation and support with the client, they will set up an appointment to discuss in detail how the agency's services can solve their problems in a strategy call. In order for a sales development rep to be successful, certain mechanics need to be in place. If there is no funnel generating a prospect list, then a sales development rep will not have anyone to call.

If there is no solid CRM in place, then there will not be inbound calls for the sales development rep to answer.

While your agency develops several marketing campaigns for your clients, you need to do the same thing for yourself. You don't want your employee sitting around doing nothing, but that may happen if there is no one to contact. That is why it's important to have a marketing associate in place before you consider bringing on a sales development rep. Sales development reps will need a steady flow of leads. Therefore, make sure that all your prerequisites are in place so that this new employee can get right to work after their initial training.

Those prerequisites include the following:

- Have an uncapped commission structure ready from day one.

- Have the process in place for your sales development associates so they can learn your process and adapt to it immediately.

- You have closed at least 15 of your own deals so far (this helps you identify your sales process).

- Build out your feeder group.

- Have your email sequences done.

- You already have a prospect list and a funnel that generates a larger list each day. The list should have at least 1500 names, and half should be from your own marketing.

- You have a CRM in place like GoHighLevel that a sales development rep can go into and make phone calls from there.

If you don't have these prerequisites in place, then review the previous few chapters about the marketing associate to help you reach that point. Until you have these mechanics in place, you won't be able to set up your sales development rep for success.

Think of the sales department you want to create as a super sports car. The sales development rep you are seeking will be placed in that sports car's driver's seat. You don't want that person to have to build the sports car for you because that isn't something they'll be able to do. Instead, they will be able to drive that sports car fast when you have your car already in place.

It's important to have these three key roles in your marketing agency to see the type of growth you've been dreaming about. But that will only happen when you can put certain mechanics into place first and hire these three key roles at particular times and phases.

As you prepare to work with a sales development rep, keep in mind that this is a long-term full-time role. In order to have long-term growth, you have to have long-term employees. You'll be working with an associate with many skill sets or someone you can train to learn these new skills for your agency. Diving into the next chapter, you'll be able to see my process of hiring, onboarding, and training a sales development rep. Finding the right talent for your agency is important, and writing the ideal job description will help you achieve that goal.

Chapter 8:

Hiring, Onboarding, and Training your Sales Development Rep (SDR)

Now that you have a good understanding of how beneficial a sales development rep can be for your agency, it's time to start the process of hiring, onboarding, and training these essential personnel on your team.

With your marketing associate off the ground and setting up your primary campaigns that are now fruitful and producing leads, the time has come to place on your team a sales development rep. That is the fuel to your fire.

When your sales development rep enters your team, they will already have a list of leads to call on. These leads are already warmed up by the marketing associate who has initiated cold outreach campaigns, Facebook ads, and retargeting campaigns that are now all connected together.

With these mechanics in place, your new sales development rep can join your agency and be able to work with the leads list to make contact. This plays an essential role in igniting growth in your agency. You can get a sales development rep for your sales team from many places. You can use online websites like Fiverr and Upwork to connect with freelancers who might be interested in working with your agency long-term.

You can also look for local employees in your area that might be willing to work alongside your team in-person instead of remotely. You could use job posting sites such as Indeed.com to find local talent to join your team.

Later on, in this chapter, you'll get to see examples of job descriptions that will be sure to attract the right sales development rep for you.

This chapter will equip you with the knowledge and know-how to hire the best sales development rep for your agency, as well as understand the importance of training your sales development rep.

Every digital marketing agency uses the same marketing techniques, but your agency is unique. It has a particular niche and processes to attract clients. Your new sales development rep will need to know these types of things, and only you or your team can provide that training.

Step One: Attracting The Right Sales Development Rep

The first thing you will do when you are getting ready to hire a sales development rep is to decide which avenue you will use to attract the right employee. You can use many websites to do this, but you have to determine if this employee will be working remotely or in your company space. Your pre-hiring checklist includes the following:

1) Determine your budget for a new employee.
2) Can you afford to hire within the US?
3) Or should you hire out of the country?

This checklist will help you determine where to start looking for your sales development rep. For example, if your agency makes around 40k a year, plus commission, then you should look offshore. If you have a high budget, then, of course, you can hire locally.

Once you decide on your budget, you know where to search for your sales development rep.

It is recommended to hire remotely, even when hiring in the USA. This allows you to keep your office environment small.

If you prefer working face-to-face with your employees in your agency's office, you can use websites like Indeed.com or LinkedIn.com to find a sales development rep who is already in your area. The work environment is more personable when you work on a small team of a few individuals. It is not a secret why small businesses like this type of environment because it enables them to be more productive.

But if you want to reach that $1 million mark in two to three years, then you will be focused on growth. There are not many small businesses that have made that type of revenue. Therefore, you have to be willing to grow your teams.

Popular websites that you've probably already used before to outsource web development, SEO, and digital content include freelance websites such as Fiverr and Upwork. Though there is a long list of potential candidates that you can easily find on these sites, these companies have many downsides. For example:

- Freelancers are usually part-time and short-term.
- They have a higher chance of bailing before a project is finished.
- Their prices vary, and cheaper doesn't always mean better.

If you have ever worked with a freelancer, you know how unpredictable they can be. Though there are freelancers who work full-time and are dedicated, these are few compared to the unpredictable ones.

To attract the right candidate, it will come down to your job description and interview process to ensure that you are hiring the best sales development rep.

Step Two: Sales Development Rep Job Description

You will be evaluating three areas once you start to receive candidates who apply to your job posting. Those three areas are:

- Experience

- Skillset
- Education

You'll have to decide if you require your future sales development rep to have an associate's or bachelor's degree and in which field. For example, most of the sales development reps at RepStack have a bachelor's degree in marketing and business, and have at least one year of experience as a sales development rep.

The sales development rep will be an important part of your agency. So, you'll want to make sure that they have some experience. However, someone with the right attitude can be trained very easily. While the sales development rep position is not very difficult, you still want to work with someone who is dedicated and a go-getter to make those connections.

The onboarding process will be a key factor in the sales development rep's success. Don't get too hung up on the person's experience because the marketing associate will have already produced the leads, and the sales development rep will be able to get started right away. Their attitude is just as important as their previous experience doing a similar job.

You want to work with someone who has a similar skillset to the tasks that you will need them to complete. But suppose a suitable candidate is missing a few skills you would like them to perform daily or weekly. In that case, you'll want to be prepared to train your new sales development rep to perform those tasks—for example, learning a new project management tool like ClickUp or a CRM tool like GoHighLevel. This is a skill set that they would need to learn to be successful.

I believe some of the most important qualities a sales development rep should possess include willingness to learn, self-motivation, and willingness to grow with the agency. If you discover these traits in a candidate from the very beginning, then you know you have a potential sales development rep.

The job requirements I normally include in a job post are as follows:

- Appointment setting experience preferred.
- Proficient skills with Google Docs, CRM systems, project management tools, cloud services, and other technology tools.
- Well-versed with technology.
- Highly organized multi-tasker and able to work on multiple instructions.
- Demonstrates excellent time management skills.
- Self-directed and able to work without supervision.
- Excellent verbal and written communication skills.
- Strong customer service and presentation skills.
- Good understanding of Digital Marketing.

For any other skills or tasks that I am looking for a sales development rep to complete, I'm prepared to train them to do that task if, by chance, they are not familiar with it. Training is a big part of bringing on any new employee, from daily performance expectations to helping the new hire understand your brand, mission, and niche.

You will need a compelling job description to attract the best sales development rep. Here are a few samples of job descriptions that you can use as a template to post your own job online.

Sales Development Rep Job Description Samples

Example #1

Looking for personality, not experience!

Hey there! We have an open position for a **sales development rep** at our company.

We geek out on things like marketing and technology, and we're growing, which is why we're looking for our next rockstar employee. In fact, we'd like to hire at least two **sales development reps** now.

Who are we looking for?

Do you love to talk to strangers on the phone and make them feel like your long-lost best friends in two seconds flat? Seriously though, can you smile and dial non-stop with absolutely zero fear of "No, we're not interested," hang-ups, and no answers? Do you have a friendly voice and an awesome attitude? If so, we'd love to talk with you.

You must be a motivated and educated young professional. We do not require much experience, but some experience is necessary.

What will you be doing?

Your mission, should you accept it (cue *Mission Impossible* theme), will be to companies across the country *(insert details about your specific agency here)* in the yard, garden, and patio industry. Examples include landscapers, lawn care providers, garden centers, and tree service companies.

You'll be working with inbound leads that will be coming from the marketing department. Your daily tasks will be calling and re-calling to confirm set appointments, as well as sending frequent emails. To accomplish this, we expect you to make 80 - 150 calls a day.

Where?

Our office in Dalles, Texas. This can be a remote or work-from-home position.

When?

8:15 am – 5:15 pm MST

How?

After training, you'll be using the CRMs that are set up for you. We expect you to keep track of your calls and record results in GoHighLevel. You'll be moving from opportunity to opportunity to make real, tangible sales.

How much?

Base hourly pays plus a commission for every listing you help claim and an additional bonus for every qualified appointment you schedule.

Some of the cool things about our company are:

- **Great People**: We have a fun team and a great company culture.

- **Great Office**: We have a great new office we just moved into with lots of room to grow. We're close to cool restaurants, Broadway Commons, and minutes from downtown Salem.

- **Innovative Tools**: We have built some of the best tools in the marketplace to help our customers with their online presence and reputation

- **Great Community**: We are very active in our local business community through the Chambers of Commerce and other groups

- **Great Opportunity To Learn**: We train — we need personality vs. experience.

- **Great Impact**: We work hard to help our customers grow their businesses. If you love helping and supporting local businesses, then this role will be perfect for you.

Next Steps?

Make no mistake! This is not an "easy" job — we are looking for a highly driven individual here.

This is a full-time position. If you're the right person for the job, fill out the form below.

We look forward to hearing from you!

Example #2

Sales Development Rep Position

We are looking for a responsible and experienced virtual sales development rep to join our team. While operating remotely, the sales assistant will make 80 to 150 calls a day. In addition, they will be expected to answer calls and emails, and assist in creating presentations and sales materials.

The ideal candidate should be tech-savvy, able to communicate through multiple channels, and be super organized.

Duties and responsibilities:

- Set appointments for the sales team
- Answer and direct phone calls
- Work within the CRM
- Manage communication and answer emails
- Prepare and organize databases and reports
- Manage social media accounts and replies

- Handles customer and employer information confidentially
- Take notes or transcribe meetings conducted online and share minutes of meetings
- Schedule meetings, manage calendar, and appointments
- Create purchase orders and track, and manage payments
- Manage filing systems, update records, and organize documentation
- Online research for materials and sources for presentations

Hands-on Experience Requirement:

- Knowledge of CRMs
- Sales, this shows us you have relationship-building skills.
- Data entry/ online research.
- Digital marketing services sales or work experience is a plus.
- Social media management is a plus.
- Understanding how websites work is a plus.
- Email management.
- Google Docs
- Basic video editing is a plus.
- Basic graphics editing using tools like Canva is a plus.
- If you have not done it, you are willing to figure it out.

Skills & Qualifications:

- Superior written and verbal communication.
- A bachelor's degree or relevant experience.
- Business Management experience would be preferred.
- Outgoing and candid personality
- Ability to work under pressure and meet deadlines.
- Proactive, solution-oriented, and out of box thinking is required for this position.
- Ability to learn new tools

Job Requirements:

This is a full-time, work-from-home-based position in the US working hours (8:00 am - 5:00 pm) EST. A basic requirement is a stable internet connection, office equipment (laptop), and a dedicated workspace. Salary: 40,000 USD - 55,000 USD based on experience and skills

Benefits: Training, referral bonus, and health insurance.

Step Three: Interviewing Sales Development Reps

Once your sales development rep job is posted, you will receive all sorts of responses. It might feel a little overwhelming in the beginning because you now have the job of weeding through all the applicants. I recommend having a team member review the applicants to help weed out the ones who apply that don't meet your requirements. Like cold calling, you have to clean up the list to focus only on promising prospects. The same thing applies to your list of applicants.

Jeff Fisher is one of RepStack's coaches and growth officers. He's a professional in the digital agency industry and in the recruiting field. He has a trick every time he posts a new job. At the end of each job posting, he leaves a question or prompting that ensures the applicant has read the entire job posting. For example, "When you apply for this job, include the word 'winner' in the heading or top of your text." This will help shortlist your candidates.

1. When you have a good list and want to start interviewing those with great potential, you can use the following questions to learn more about a candidate and ensure they will be a good fit for you. **Tell me a little about yourself.**
2. Where are you from?
3. What are your hobbies?
4. What's important to you?
5. What were you doing most recently? Why did you leave?
6. What are your strengths?
7. What do you feel you do best?
8. What type of work have you done with others in the past?
9. What does your work environment look like? Do you have a quiet, dedicated place to work? Do you have high-speed internet? What about your computer?

10. What interested you in this position?

11. Are you looking for a short-term or long-term role?

12. If we contacted your last employer & asked them to rate you on a scale of 1-10 (with 1 being terrible & 10 being the best), what would they rate you & why?

Keep in mind these details and other bits of information about your agency that you want to share with a potential candidate to see their response.

- Let the candidate know, "If you choose to work with our agency, all the above questions are pre-verified during multiple vetting interviews."

- Share your agency's mission, niche, and target audience to see if they have experience in your niche.

- Review their availability and whether they can work with your time zones.

As you review the possible interview questions, add to the list a few questions of your own that you'd want to ask a potential candidate.

I recommend scheduling video calls using programs such as Zoom so you can see the candidate and be able to read their body language. Sometimes that can tell you more about a person than what they say. Since most sales development reps work remotely, this is also a perfect time to test their internet connection and computer programs. They can share their screen with you during the interview to show what websites and programs they are already familiar with.

You can test your candidate by having them complete a typing test, or you can have them read a sales script to you and do a bit of role-playing. You can act as a potential client, and the candidate can pretend to be doing either a cold or warm call. This allows you to see how they work in action during the interview process.

At RepStack, we hire candidates with the intention that there will be a training phase. When clients come to us for associates, they are ready to go because they are already vetted and trained. Here is an example Loom video of a RepStack associate. This video can serve as a benchmark for your candidate.

Another thing you can do that Jeff Fisher does is ask your candidate to complete a pre-hiring video that they will then send to you. You can learn a lot about them when they are willing to do a video of themselves as part of the hiring process. Those who are not willing to do this will give you an idea that they are not worth your time and will not be dedicated to your agency.

Step Four: Onboarding and Training Your Sales Development Rep

Once the interviews are all said and done, you'll be left with one or two sales development reps with which you are ready to start. This is an exciting time for your agency because you are about to start booking more sales calls.

But just like with a marketing associate, you'll have to spend some time onboarding and training your sales development rep. Or, you can delegate this responsibility to your sales team lead, manager, or supervisor.

The bottom line is that your new sales development rep isn't going to know everything about your agency right away. They'll need time to review your website, products, services, and target audience. There is an onboarding process where the sales development rep will have time to learn everything about your agency as though they've been working with you for years.

Though a sales development representative will have experience with inbound and outbound calls, they might need training on how to manage your CRM like GoHighLevel. You might organize tasks and have mechanics set up differently than their last employer had.

Keep in mind that your new sales development rep will require some training to function 100% on their own. This is a part of automating your digital marketing agency so you can step back and relax. One of the major things you want to make clear to your new hire is your expectations. Here are my expectations from all our associates:

1. **Responsiveness**: Be quick to reply when I send a message and be on top of the ball. To me, that is the most important aspect of this role. If I send a message during work hours and don't hear back quickly, I will question how engaged you are in the position.

2. **Be resourceful**: I'll share with you what needs to be done but if you are stuck on something, try to solve it yourself before asking another team member or me. If it's something you could have solved by contacting support or doing a Google search first, then do that.

3. **Honesty**: Just be honest & forthcoming in all our dealings.

4. **Innovate**: We are an extremely fast-growing business. As you go about your job, we want you to find ways to improve things, make suggestions, and enhance the way we operate.

5. **Work hard**: There is a lot to do. I'll need you by my side, proactively learning, innovating, and getting things done.

6. **Ask for help**: If you need direction, resources, or support, don't hesitate to ask. I want you to be happy, clear, and fulfilled in your role.

Making your expectations clear to your sales development rep is very important. They need to know who to contact when they have questions, but also give them the freedom to search out those answers before they start asking questions.

Onboarding Checklist

- What tools need to be set up for them? Who will set those up? Create a checklist.

- What will their orientation process look like?
    - Initial Day
    - Accessing Tools / Software
    - Communication Expectations

- How will they be trained in what you expect them to do?
    - Orientation on the roll
    - Training on the day-to-day

- What will they be expected to report daily/weekly/monthly?

- How will you gauge their performance?

- Communicate the expectations.

- INITIAL DAY
- ACCESSING TOOLS / SOFTWARE
- COMMUNICATION EXPECTATIONS
- HOW WILL THEY BE TRAINED IN WHAT YOU EXPECT THEM TO DO?
- ORIENTATION ON THE ROLL
- TRAINING ON THE DAY-TO-DAY
- WHAT WILL THEY BE EXPECTED TO REPORT DAILY/WEEKLY / MONTHLY?
- HOW WILL YOU GAUGE THEIR PERFORMANCE?
- COMMUNICATE THE EXPECTATIONS!

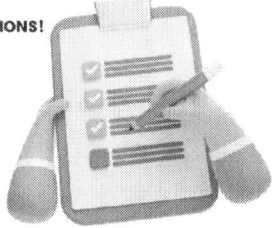

With my company RepStack, I use an ongoing training, management, and accountability process for all our associates. It answers the questions of "When will they meet with you for feedback?" and "How will you continue to train and develop your associates?"

Below are RepStack-only processes, but you should have something similar present:

→ Continuous training inside our Training Academy | RepStack Success Academy

→ Custom training courses from World Class Business Coaches such as:

- ◆ Josh Nelson | Seven Figure Agency
- ◆ Andrew Cass | PipelinePRO
- ◆ Alex Schlinsky | Prospecting on Demand

◆ Dennis Yu | BlitzMetrics

→ Weekly Associate Check-ins

→ Monthly Client Check-ins

→ Time Tracking Application: RepStack uses Time Doctor, while Upwork uses its native software.

→ Tracking EOD reports

■ Update daily agenda on CRM.

■ Follow up and send reminders to prospects who have booked a strategy session

■ Follow up with leads generated from inbound marketing

　　■ START OFF BY DIALING THE INBOUND AND OUTBOUND CALLS OF THE DAY.
　　　● DIAL VIRTUAL HIRING GUIDE OPT-INS
　　　● NO SHOW ON DISCOVERY CALL LEADS
　　　● DIAL PARTIALLY QUALIFIED LEADS
　　　● DIAL CHASE-UP LEADS

HEY AGENCY OWNER, THIS IS ME THE SALES AND DEVELOPMENT REPRESENTATIVE AT REPSTACK. I WILL TELL YOU HOW AND WHAT I DO IN A DAY. LET'S GET STARTED!

It is important to have an onboarding, training, management, and accountability process all set up for your new hires. This ensures that your sales development rep is prepared for their role with your agency, and will continue to grow as your agency does.

Not only are you putting these young individuals on a path to kickstart their careers, but these sales development reps will also earn your agency a lot of money because they are eager to learn and show off their skill set. Putting into place the commission aspect of their job will inspire the sales development rep to reach new heights.

Chapter 9:

Successful SDR Case Studies

I have so many great case studies for sales development reps because they are a driving force for any digital marketing agency. In this chapter, I highlight some of the most amazing stories that have come my way.

I've learned from hearing the success stories of fellow agency owners that their sales development reps have become integral parts of their agencies. The SDR might start off as an appointment setter, but within months they are taking on bigger roles. This includes helping with sales presentations.

It is true that sales development reps need to be trained and taken seriously in order to aspire to remain long-term employees. Be aware that there is always a bit of a learning curve for any new hire at a growing digital marketing agency.

But these full-time team members can flourish and grow in an agency with SOPs and a feedback loop set up for their employees. In the beginning, new hires need consistent feedback to set them up for long-term success. What you'll discover in these case studies is that sales development reps make a big difference in an agency with mechanics already in place. They can take on a wide variety of roles and tasks, causing the agency to function with little intervention from the owner.

By delegating these tasks to a skilled SDR that is dedicated and self-motivated, you'll discover in these case studies how continued growth in the sales department happens *within* an agency. By helping your sales development rep to flourish as you do, you'll be able to continue to grow as an agency.

How a Kitchen Remodeling SEO Owner Landed More Clients With A Sales Development Rep

REPSTACK CASE STUDY

HE IS ONE OF THE FASTEST LEARNERS I'VE EVER SEEN IN MY LIFE.

MIKE GOLDSTEIN | NOUFEL

Working with Michael Goldstein, owner of Kitchen Remodeling SEO, is a true honor. He is a man of many talents who is a true entrepreneur. After learning about his journey to the success he has now, it is clear that he has the drive and inspires all his employees to have that same motivation.

This is Michael's story.

"After realizing that I was not going to make it as a professional basketball player (I wasn't even close), I spent many evenings trawling the local press and online job boards looking for the dream role that was out of reach."

"So, it is no surprise that I now work in two industries that reward me for helping people and small businesses realize their potential and setting them on their way to achieving profitable success."

"I am a man who wears two hats, one as an SEO analyst and copywriter, and one as an attorney. I am Google Analytics Certified and the founding member of several companies, including VRG Web Design, and one of the founding members and a Partner at the Law Office of Goldstein and Clegg, LLC."

"Writing is not only a critical element of my profession but also quite enjoyable to me. With that in mind, I have been granted the opportunity to become a published author, as well as an advocate for my clients."

"My work has been featured on Moody's Analytics website as well as in the University of Massachusetts Southern New England Law Journal and has been quoted by bankrate.com and Boston.com on several occasions."

"I was a co-host of the weekly radio program, Consumer Debt Radio, airing on 1510 AM, WWZN-Boston, in addition to being heard on the Money Matters Radio Network several times on 1120 AM in Boston, and on the Sporting News Radio Network in the Boston market, discussing web development and SEO strategy."

"Recently, I have launched a podcast discussing tips and strategies relative to Local SEO."

"On a personal note, I would like to think of myself as a dedicated father and husband who also taught at the college level for many years at Merrimack College in North Andover, Massachusetts."

After reading Michael's story, you might be thinking, "Why does he need a sales development rep if he's already had so much success?"

The truth is that you haven't really built a digital marketing agency until your sales process is automated. This means that sales are happening even when the owner is not involved in the day-to-day tasks. Having an SDR at the beginning of your processes is the first step in building an independent agency. Michael wants to lay the groundwork for an SDR to join the team. Then, he can step back and let the sales roll in without having to manage every process. The process becomes an automatic happening each day that continues to grow his agency.

This is a game changer, especially when a sales development rep is dedicated and is able to put their best into the agency. While many virtual assistants divide their time between the many agencies they work for, offering a full-time position to a sales development rep guarantees you'll have a dedicated employee.

When I talked to Michael about his recent experience with his new sales development rep, he had some pretty amazing things to say about Noufel.

"The sales development rep that was recently placed with us has been outstanding. He's one of the fastest learners I've ever seen in my life. He picked up how to use Loom for SEO audits after I worked with him for about two hours, teaching him how to do it."

"Now he's been reaching out to clients and has been able to generate several conversations with prospective clients. Through this, he's been booking strategy sessions for us. I look forward to the agency's future with Noufel on board."

There are so many new technologies available out there, and this story shows how something as simple as a Loom video can lead to generating sales. To truly understand this forward-thinking way of landing clients, I took the time to talk with Noufel to see what his process was. It's pretty amazing what he's able to do to land new clients for his agency.

"To start my day, I begin with recording five to six Loom videos where I will review a potential client's website, blog, or social media and point out where the SEO could be improved. In the video, I'll show the client how they can increase their marketing and the different strategies they could use." "Normally, after they have been emailed or messaged to the client, these videos will result in a strategy call. Prospects really like to visibly see how the agency can solve their problems instead of them having to imagine it for themselves. For me, it's a pretty simple thing to do, and I enjoy creating those solutions and showcasing them in Loom videos."

"In addition to those videos, I also call prospects from the list generated through the agency's key campaigns and funnels. There are lead magnets and different campaigns running right now that generate a list, I can go through every day to make contact and book more discovery and strategy calls."

"I really enjoy making videos and will often make promotional videos for the agency as well. While I do focus on making sales for the agency, there are marketing tasks that I enjoy completing.

Sometimes, I'll even update the website or the agency's portfolio as some of my daily tasks."

After speaking with Noufel, it's clear why he's such a great match for Michael and his agency. He's just equally as talented and able to take on all sorts of tasks. Anything that Michael needs to teach him, Noufel is able to pick up right away and start utilizing.

It is Michael's frequent feedback and up-to-date training that makes Noufel such a great sales development rep. He's motivated to do his best and dedicated to the agency. He has long-term plans with Michael and doesn't plan to work with any other agency.

Since Noufel has taken over the task of creating Loom videos for prospective clients, something he was able to learn quickly and clearly enjoys doing, Michael has seen his agency blooming. He has plans to put Noufel into a management position so he can teach the other sales development reps to do the same task.

With this first SDR hire, Michael has been able to lay the groundwork for building his sales department. With Noufel soon in a management position, he will, in turn, be able to hire and train new sales development reps. This part of Michael's agency will be able to run without the need for his interference.

How Service Legend Was Able To Increase Sales With Their Sales Executive

REPSTACK CASE STUDY

HE IS AN ABSOLUTE TOP PERFORMING EMPLOYEE. COULDN'T HAVE ASKED FOR A BETTER EMPLOYEE COMING FROM REPSTACK.

KRISTIN DAVIS | MANNAN MASOOD

The stories I love to hear from fellow agency owners are the ones where their new associates are put into executive positions because of their performance. This is one such case with Ryan and Kristin Davis, owners of Davis Construction Marketing.

They began working with Mannan, who proved to be a wonderful asset to their agency, making it an essay choice to move him into an executive position within the sales department.

When talking with Ryan, he gave me the backstory of how he was able to slide into digital marketing based on the solutions he provided for the company he was already working with.

"Before I jumped headfirst into the marketing business, I was actually in the Concrete Coating and painting business myself as a Sales and Marketing Manager for Steve Holloway Painting in Bakersfield, California (He was our first client). I led that company's digital marketing efforts, did commercial estimating, and even ran estimated appointments and closed deals in the home. I helped grow that company to being consistently 8-10 weeks booked out every month.

"I thought to myself, 'Could I help other concrete coating and painting companies across the country get this busy?'"

"So, I asked the owner if he would be my first client for my new business… he said YES!"

"I then started doing the same thing for other concrete coating and painting companies all over the United States, and now we have a team of 6 and growing. We produce 1,000s of leads every month on demand for our clients and free them from the devastation of not having new customers coming in the door on demand."

"I'm even a co-owner (with my family) of a concrete coating business here in Arizona, we're actually a Penntek dealer. We help Concrete Coating & Painting companies get to the next level using our Concrete Coating & Painting Online Sales System."

Ryan has shown how easy it is to become a digital marketing agency owner when you have experience in the niche you are focusing on. This is a great story of how he saw solutions for the company he was already working for and then was able to replicate those solutions for other construction companies.

As Ryan and his wife Kristin started their own digital marketing agency, they needed help from an experienced sales development rep. Someone who could take all their leads and make deals. While Ryan and Kristin were great at marketing, they needed extra help with all the leads they were generating.

That's when they met Mannan. He started out with Davis Construction Marketing as an appointment setter. But when Ryan and Kristin realized how talented he was and the type of results he was able to create, they quickly promoted him to sales executive.

Kristin had this to say about her experience working with Mannan. "Mannan works hand in hand with the business development department and the sales department. He makes a lot of outgoing calls to all our US-based clients, and he is an absolute top-notch employee."

"We couldn't ask for a better employee because of his high performance. He's stellar all the way around. We never have to worry if a task was completed or a certain call was made because he keeps constant communication through Slack."

"We're so grateful for such a high-quality employee with a great personality."

As this story shows, there are many aspects to what makes a great sales development rep. It's not only their dedication and ability to be a high performer but small things such as personality and ease of working with them. Communication is key to any project, and being able to have frequent communication ensures everyone is on the same page. Curious to know what Mannan does every day as a sales executive, I took the time to catch up with him to get a better idea of what his day looks like while working remotely.

He explained, "Every day, I follow a similar routine for tackling my responsibilities for the day. But the very first thing I do is log on to Slack to say hello to my sales team. Then, I'll review my emails to ensure there isn't an important email I need to take care of right away."

"Next, I'll move onto the schedule of discovery calls. I'll look at the following day and contact those clients using GoHighLevel to confirm those appointments with the clients. Once I've qualified them, I'll move them into the discovery calls list."

"I'll then move onto the New Leads list to contact those prospective clients before speaking with the prospects who have downloaded the agency's checklist. I enjoy qualifying new clients for a discovery call and booking those appointments. This is one of the funnels that generate a new prospect list every day." "On GoHighLevel, there is also a list of "no answers." These are clients who were scheduled for a discovery call in the past week but didn't answer their phones during the scheduled time. My goal with this list is to give them a callback, get them on the phone, and rebook that discovery call."

"One of the things I enjoy is being part of the discovery calls. I'm there to assist Danny, who is my lead. After the calls, I will update all the trackers to indicate if the discovery call turned into a strategy call, was booked for a strategy call, or the client wasn't qualified in the end."

"A handful of other tasks I keep an eye on are any sales messages on GoHighLevel that need to be delegated to the sales team. We are also beginning a new cold DMing campaign to send messages through social media, which I will soon be leading."

Mannan has grown so much after joining the Davis Construction Marketing team. Having started out as a sales development rep, he's quickly moved up the ladder to an executive. Now he is managing his own sales team, delegating assignments, while maintaining his responsibilities.

He's not only booking discovery calls but participating in them as well. It's clear to see how he is helping the agency become more automated, allowing Ryan and Kristin to focus more time on raising a family together while still remaining successful.

Some of the unique things about Manna is that he is dedicated to the agency he works for. He's a full-time, remote employee who enjoys the work that he gets to do each day. In return, he receives continued education and learning opportunities so he can help create new campaigns, such as cold DMing on social media.

SDR 2.0s: The Future of Sales Development Reps

I've learned from working with sales development reps that they become the gatekeepers of any digital marketing agency. By hiring the SDR that is working with the sales department team — doing database activity and reactivation, OP ends, book funnels, calling the missed appointments list — what you're going to discover in time, as I have, is that they become what I have termed the SDR 2.0.

Digital marketing agency owners have begun to sell some of the hours of their sales development reps to their clients to help take care of their tasks. Sometimes they offer this as a free service to sell other marketing packages to their clients. What these SDR 2.0s do is contact all the leads for the client and book appointments. This is certainly going above and beyond when it comes to what an SDR can do for you and your clients.

The quality of leads has always been an issue that clients complain about. But the issue is not the quality of leads. It is the quality of the sales team. When a sales team doesn't book follow-up appointments, get back to leads fast enough, and offer wonderful customer service, then that lead will not make a purchase.

It is in this situation that database reactivation needs to happen. That is why digital marketing agency owners are lending out their SDR 2.0s to make changes happen for their clients. These new and improved SDRs are not cold callers (and you'd be a fool to call them that). They are business-educated individuals with a degree in marketing and business, and amazing communication skills. I've learned that sales development reps are capable of more than their initial hired tasks. They are capable of being campaign managers and training new associates. Not only are they able to help manage your leads, but they can do it for multiple clients. Invest in your SDRs by challenging them and providing opportunities for future growth. This is the new and upcoming trends in the digital marketing agency industry. SDRs are so much more than what they used to be. It takes the right SDR to be motivated and willing to grow into these new positions and responsibilities.

Chris Johnson is doing a wonderful job at this with his business model, SDR concierge. He has a mentor and coaching business that can use this new concept successfully. Most of my clients are doing something very similar because they know how it sparks massive growth in their agencies. This is truly the first step in your agency's process of becoming fully automated.

Chapter 10:

Secret 3 Unlocked: The Account Manager

With both the marketing and sales development rep in place for your marketing agency, you'll see all sorts of growth in your agency within 6 to 12 months. With the key campaigns and funnels in place, your sales development rep has plenty of prospects to call each day.

But as new clients start rolling in and revenue increases, you might notice another problem. While you might not have to worry so much about creating new marketing campaigns or reaching out to all your prospects, you now have a full list of new clients to stay with your agency for the long run. Most importantly, as new clients sign up for your services, you don't want current or previous clients slipping out the back door. That will just create a vicious circle. You want to be able to bring in new clients while retaining the current ones for as long as possible.

Instead of being bogged down with these tasks, there is a third key role that you can put in place for your agency to take the weight off your shoulders. That third key role is the account manager.

The number one reason why clients leave is perceived indifference. You, as the agency owner, cannot be everywhere at the same time. The account manager is the person to give your clients 24/7 access to you without you needing to be on the call with the client. They can overcommunicate with the client, so you don't have to. An account manager's responsibilities and abilities are truly endless as they focus on communication and happy clients. This individual can take on a list of current clients and is responsible for retaining them for as long as possible. They coordinate with all the fulfillment teams while keeping the client updated. They are your voice, so you don't have to constantly talk to clients to retain them. With this last key role in place about 90 days after your sales development rep joined, you'll have a fully functioning marketing agency that runs on its own. You'll be able to monitor your agency's progress from your computer or Smartphone while focusing on your agency's strategic growth.

Imagine being able to step away from the office when you need to, and worry less about whether your new client has been taken care of. Or the stress of managing your current clients and worrying your fulfillment team won't create the content in time.

There is much that an account manager can do for you. In this chapter, I'll review all the tasks that an account manager can take on while providing the latest examples of what account managers are doing today for their agencies.

What An Account Manager Can Do For You

An account manager is someone who is an excellent communicator. With their attention to detail and great customer service, they can provide clients with everything they need and purchase from your agency. They are highly committed to client satisfaction and often thrive in an account management career. An account manager's attentiveness to the needs of those they represent can be the difference between a happy customer who maintains a long-term relationship with the company and an unhappy one who takes their business elsewhere.

Account manager responsibilities include:

- Developing long-term relationships with a portfolio of clients.
- Connecting with key business executives and stakeholders to continue long-term relationships and continued renewal of services.
- A liaison between customers and cross-functional internal teams to ensure the timely and successful delivery of all the solutions you offer.
- Manage and develop client accounts to start and maintain favorable relationships with clients.

- Responsible for leading a team of other account managers dedicated to meeting their assigned clients' operational needs.

- Collect client testimonials

- Grow the account by making upsells

From an overview perspective, an account manager becomes your voice and face with the current clients they are assigned. They ensure all the client's purchased solutions and services are completed. And if a client has an issue with anything, they contact their account manager. **Not you.** This frees up a lot of your time and lowers your stress levels immensely.

Account managers are the customer service department for your agency. They answer all of the emails from current clients, arranging weekly follow-up meetings, and even monthly meetings to see if there is anything else the client needs. They are not only ensuring the current service package is fulfilled but also ensuring the current clients continue to make purchases by pitching new services.

The *number one thing* that an account manager will be able to accomplish is developing trusting relationships with all major clients to ensure they don't turn to your competition.

Think for a moment about a strong trust-based relationship you have with another business. It might be a certain member of your bank or even the barista at the coffee shop you stop into every morning.

When you create a trusting relationship with someone else, you don't feel like you're doing business. It feels more like you are working with a friend and someone you can trust your money and business with.

That type of feeling is what an account manager can do for your agency. It goes beyond the tasks they are able to complete each day and the list of client projects they oversee. It's the customer service and relationship responsibilities that make these employees a key role in your agency's growth.

A full list of responsibilities that you could expect your account manager to complete can include the following:

- Acquire a thorough understanding of key customer needs and requirements.
- Expand the relationships with existing customers by continuously proposing solutions that meet their objectives – such as website reviews, marketing campaigns, and social media rebranding.
- Ensure the correct products and services are delivered to customers in a timely manner.
- Serve as the link of communication between key customers and internal teams.
- Resolve any customer issues and problems and deal with complaints to maintain trust.
- Play an integral part in generating new sales that will turn into long-lasting relationships.
- Prepare regular progress reports and forecasts for internal and external stakeholders using key account metrics.
- Collect valuable client testimonials such as videos for marketing and Google reviews for future clients to review.

As you are beginning to see, an account manager is essential in keeping your client communication at an all-time high. No more will you have to worry about remembering to schedule a follow-up meeting with your client or being in meetings all day with clients.

You'll have one or more account managers to handle every communication aspect with your clients so you can turn your focus on other tasks.

Overcommunication Using Account Managers is Great for Business

Every year, new changes in the digital marketing industry are happening. Whether they are social media advertising rules or new platforms that are offering advertising space, new trends are happening all the time.

It's important to be up-to-date with all these changes, but with so many responsibilities, it's sometimes hard to stay current with all the trends. This is another reason why account managers are such a vital part of a growing agency.

They are able to spot these changes based on the feedback from your clients. When clients ask for a new service they've seen from a competitor, it's time for you to decide if your agency will be offering the same service.

Or, when there are new advertising policies on all the social media platforms, you can rely on your account manager to relay the news back to the client. Now you'll have more than just yourself to stay on top of all the changes in advertising.

Examples of targets and benchmarks you can expect from your account manager include the following:

- Retaining current agency accounts every month.
- Keeping up on trends, changes, and competitor actions that might affect the client, i.e., social media policy changes, advertising rules, etc.
- Making upsells.
- Collecting client reviews.
- Holding regular review meetings with clients.
- Acting as a liaison between the client and your agency – conveying information, and ensuring a smooth lead-flow process, while managing client accounts.
- Making the client aware of other services and actions that may lead to greater success – Upsells.
- Monitoring the client's budget, explaining costs, and negotiating new terms if necessary.
- Negotiating contracts and closing agreements to maximize profits.
- Providing progress reports to clients and upper management.
- Growing current accounts.

This list gives you an idea of how you'll be able to track your account manager's progress. As long as they can maintain these target benchmarks each month, you know you've found the perfect employee to join your team.

Successful agencies need to be able to provide customers with the best possible service. That means hiring elite account managers. In the next chapter, you'll be able to review how to hire the perfect account manager for your agency.

The Right Time To Hire An Account Manager

As an agency owner, I had no trouble hiring web developers, SEO professionals, and technical people for the fulfillment part of the agency. However, we tend to delay hiring these three key roles — especially the account manager. Until I started to learn how to offload tasks from my plate, I struggled to grow my agency. Why is that?

For a long time, you've been the one who has been managing all your clients, ensuring smooth sailing. After all, you want continued revenue. Not just a one-time client.

You might enjoy closing the deal with clients because of the rush of satisfaction it gives you. But the sooner you are able to delegate the majority of the tasks and responsibilities discussed earlier in this chapter, the sooner you'll have the growth you've been dreaming about for your agency.

For the longest time, I felt like I needed an extra set of hands within the first few years of managing my own digital marketing agency. I heard the same thing being said by fellow agency owners.

It wasn't until I hired an account manager to help me manage all the tasks associated with fulfilling client requests that I was able to see my agency enter explosive growth mode. Having that extra set of hands made all the difference in the world.

Remember, the number one reason why clients leave is perceived indifference. As an agency owner, you can't be there for your clients all the time. Shifting between marketing, sales, and being an account manager is not possible for long-term growth. You're going to become burnt out and stretched thin.

You can prevent this from happening by placing an account manager on your team. Their sole responsibility is to retain clients every month.

Every digital marketing agency needs these three key roles. If you are currently making at least $10,000 a month, then you can start thinking about placing these key roles (start with the marketing associate if you have less monthly revenue). There is a list of different ways to find and hire an account manager that will fit your budget.

> *Account management for agency owners is normally the last thing they can let go of and delegate to someone else.*

Account management for agency owners is normally the last thing they can let go of and delegate to someone else. We often feel that we need to be involved with every single client. To be there every time the client calls in. We feel that every time a client sends in an email, we have to reply to it ourselves because perhaps we were the ones to have closed the deal, or we know them personally. As soon as you have more than five clients, you'll want to consider bringing on board an account manager.

Digital marketing agency owners are good at a lot of things. They are leading an enterprise offering digital marketing solutions. But you won't be able to do it all yourself without getting burnt out and thinking of going back to your day job.

Having an account manager can be a hard task to take on because you feel the need to manage your clients. But delegating these tasks and not having to be worried about being pulled in so many directions will give you peace of mind and allow your agency to grow.

When you are able to step back, you'll gain more time on your hands and will be able to reinvest that time in other areas of your life or business. With these three key roles in place, you'll be able to watch from a distance instead of needing to be in the thick of it each day.

At the beginning of my agency days, it was a love/hate relationship for me to always take care of my clients. I felt the need to always be there for them to solve their problems. But it was very difficult for me to do it 24/7.

I trained myself that as soon as a client sent me a message, I would immediately reply. I would take care of their issues right away by assigning the task to the web development team or the marketing campaign designer. Whatever the client needed, I was quick to make it happen.

And it was exhausting to do this every day. Do you feel like you can relate to this experience?

In the beginning, I didn't realize that an account manager could do all of that for me. More so, they could do a much better job than I could because they were dedicating their full day to that one role while I was being pulled into all sorts of directions.

An account manager is prepared to take care of your clients and provide customer service at a world-class level.

> *Often agency owners think that they need to be involved in every aspect of client interaction in order to have a successful agency. But that isn't the truth.*

Often agency owners think that they need to be involved in every aspect of client interaction in order to have a successful agency. But that isn't the truth. The solution is to hire someone who is well-versed in account management. They can live and breathe the values of your agency. With a little bit of training, they can take on interacting with your clients full-time, so you don't have to. While you are often pulled in many directions between marketing, sales, and account management, your account manager can focus on the sole task of retaining your clients for you.

Some of the superpowers that account managers have are their ability to focus on the same details that a client is requesting. While agency owners are normally really good at talking and selling, an account manager can get the details of a client's problem and quickly find a solution.

Account managers can follow through with all the agency's clients. They can communicate, ensure that the task is being completed with the team, and then get back to the client to report that the work has been completed.

When you are working on particular projects for your agency, you don't want to be stopped right in the middle of what you are doing to handle a client's problem, either with their website or to start working with them for a new marketing campaign. Yes, it's great to have continued business, but you can delegate that communication aspect to an account manager so that you can remain focused on your own priorities. I love working with my account managers today because they can handle all clients' issues. They want more leads from social media. They want to book more customers every month. No matter the client's problem, the account manager can talk with them on a personal level to solve those problems and continue to retain that client. All my account managers know the importance of creating interpersonal relationships with their assigned clients. They often have monthly one-on-one meetings with the clients to review any concerns and ensure there are few issues.

One of the things I find interesting about my account managers is that in order to create those personal relationships, they talk about more than just business in their monthly meetings. They're also catching up with each other's personal lives. This is how strong relationships are built.

In turn, account managers are always improving their customer service skills and teaching those skills to their teams. Account managers are not only the customer service hub for current clients but also coach the digital marketing teams they manage in order to fulfill the services the clients purchase. They not only create a strong personal relationship with the agency's clients but also with their team members. A diverse group of creative content is being produced, and an account manager will oversee that production every day.

One of the account managers with RepStack is currently managing 20 clients. Yet, every agency is different. Where one agency might have an account manager managing 15 clients, I have seen some agencies have each account manager covering 30 clients—managing that many clients require a well-laid-out SOP system. Overall, the biggest benefit of working with an account manager is their ability to retain clients and upsell. That is the bottom-line purpose of their position, making this associate a vital part of an agency's growth.

It's one thing to have clients. It's another to keep those clients long-term. When you start working with an account manager, you will be surprised by the results and the stress relief you will experience.

Chapter 11:

Hiring, Onboarding, and Training Your Account Manager

Each of the three key roles is unique in the tasks they will complete each day for your agency. Out of all three, the account manager is the most important. They can take on a wide range of tasks and be a major component in your agency's customer service department.

Hiring an account manager is a hard task to accomplish. First, because as agency owners, it's the position that is often hard to let go of. You're more tempted to manage your clients instead of letting that task go to someone else.

The second reason why hiring an account manager is a hard task is that you want to hire an account manager with experience and top-notch communication skills. Not only someone who can speak clearly and eloquently but also a fast thinker who can resolve problems and provide quick solutions.

With an account manager playing such a vital role in your agency's growth, you might be concerned about finding the right individual for the job. This chapter will dive into the three parts of acquiring a new account manager. First, you'll learn how to hire the right individual for the job with sample job descriptions and postings that you'll be able to use right away from this book.

Then, you'll get to read about the unique process of onboarding an account manager. You want to prepare the right candidate for their role at your agency. You'll have to decide if you are going to personally onboard the account manager, or have one of your team leads or supervisors do that for you.

Finally, you'll have to train your account manager. Not only does your account manager need to learn your agency's mission and brand, but they also need to gain continuing education to stay on top of the latest trends. While some agency owners might not have thought about investing in training, you'll soon discover why continued training will take you to that $1 million mark in 2-3 years.

Hiring An Account Manager

Hiring the right person to be your account manager is vital. While posting job descriptions and ads might be a hassle, the examples in this part of the chapter will help you attract the right individual for your agency.

As in previous chapters, when it comes to hiring remote associates, you have options of where you're going to start looking. You might want someone local who can work alongside you in the office. So, make that decision now if you want your account manager to physically come into the office each day or if you are comfortable with this individual being remote.

If you are looking for an in-person account manager who will show up at the company office, then you'll want to use platforms like Indeed.com, LinkedIn.com, ziprecruiter.com, etc.

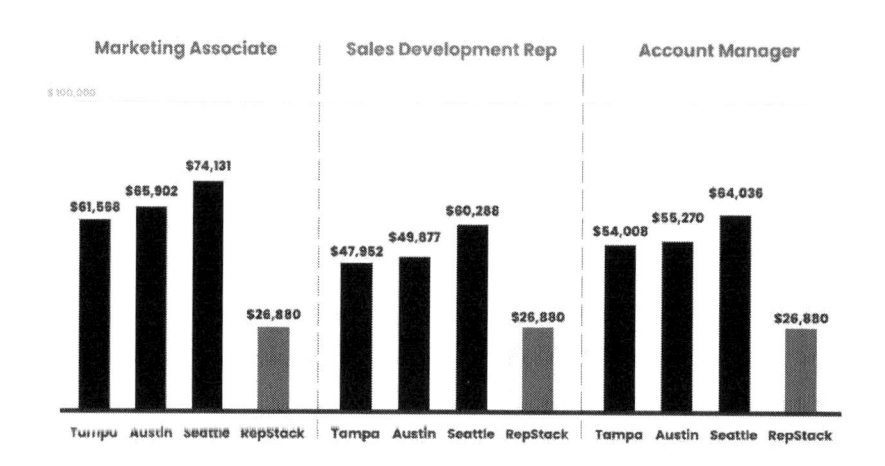

	Marketing Associate	Sales Development Rep	Account Manager
Tampa	$61,588	$47,952	$54,008
Austin	$65,902	$49,877	$55,270
Seattle	$74,131	$60,288	$64,036
RepStack	$26,880	$26,880	$26,880

I personally like to use LinkedIn.com to do a background check on an employee's work history, while Indeed.com is great for weeding through applications by reviewing their resume first, so it matches your requirements.

Suppose you are comfortable with your account manager working remotely. In that case, your pool of candidates will be much greater as you consider connecting with potential account managers from around the world. Hiring outside of your country has many benefits, from affordable salaries to less tax paperwork. Since the minimum wage is lower in some countries, you'd be surprised how much money you can save working with many experienced professionals from countries like the Philippines, Bangladesh, Pakistan, etc.

To find remote talent, you can use websites such as Fiverr and Up Work to find all sorts of talent. You've probably used these websites to find web developers and SEO specialists in the past. But you can also use these sites to find account managers.

The only downside to these sites is that you will receive an overwhelming response to your job post almost instantly. It will take some time to weed through all the applicants, so consider having a team lead to assist you with reviewing the applications before creating a list of individuals you'd actually like to hire.

To get you started, here are example job descriptions for the perfect account manager that you can use and customize right away.

Example One

Job Opening for Account Manager (Digital Marketing) (Remote)

About Our Company

RepStack is on a mission to innovate the hiring and working style. We help agencies onboard the best virtual associates, handpicked according to the needs of our clients. An account manager will handle client accounts with a smooth integration process in minimal time.

We are looking for a skilled Key Account Manager to oversee the company's relationships with its most important clients. You will be responsible for obtaining and maintaining long-term key customers by comprehending their requirements.

The ideal candidate will be apt in building strong relationships with strategic customers. You will be able to identify needs and requirements to promote our company's solutions and achieve mutual satisfaction. The goal is to contribute to sustaining and growing our business to achieve long-term success.

Responsibilities:

- Maintain high levels of client satisfaction through virtual assistant success management.
- As the voice of the client, identify trends, needs, or challenges and escalate these to the appropriate department.
- Identify and coordinate communications between customers and appropriate internal resources.
- Provide consistent, accurate, and timely communication to clients through verbal and written correspondence.
- Maintain client files accurately and consistently documenting conversations.

Requirements

- Exceptional English communication skills along with linguistics for US and Canadian clients (US accent preferable).
- Minimum of one year experience in client-facing roles (preferably with US clients).
- Time management, relationship building, and organizational skills

- Outgoing and candid personality while being people-oriented.
- Willingness to learn and grow in this role.

What's in it for you?

- Work from the comfort of your home and save the stress of commuting.
- A career path that will open a lot of opportunities.
- A chance to work with international clients and learn what they are practicing.
- Job security.
- Health insurance, gratuity, and bonuses.

Some of the things I'd like to point out about this sample job description are the key elements that will ensure you are attracting the right candidates. First, it's important to clearly point out their responsibilities, as well as the requirements they must meet. For RepStack, it's important for our associates to have experience, be willing to learn, and have exceptional English communication.

Now the part of this job description that will ensure I receive plenty of outstanding candidates for an account manager position is the part labeled "what's in it for you?" You want an account manager who is willing to work full-time and dedicated solely to your agency without working for other agencies at the same time or even moonlighting.

Therefore, you will have to offer your account manager perks that will keep them with your agency, such as health insurance and a career path. Offering these to your remote team members will ensure that they stick with your agency instead of spreading themselves thin between multiple agencies.

As you create your own job description, take the time to be descriptive with your list of responsibilities and requirements. In the interview phase, you'll also use this list to ensure that your ideal candidate can really do those tasks, either by providing evidence of previous experience or by roleplaying during the interview.

Here is the list of responsibilities and requirements I use when posting a job for an account manager:

Skills & Requirements

- Proven work experience as an Account Manager.
- Demonstrable ability to communicate, present, and influence key stakeholders at all levels of an organization.
- Solid experience with CRM software (GoHighLevel, Zoho CRM, or HubSpot) and MS Office (particularly MS Excel).
- Experience delivering client-focused solutions to customer needs.
- Proven ability to juggle multiple account management projects simultaneously while maintaining sharp attention to detail.
- Excellent listening, negotiation, and presentation abilities.
- Strong verbal and written communication skills.

- BA/BS degree in Business Administration, Sales, or a relevant field.

Roles, Duties & Expectations

- Meet with clients at least once per month to review reports, progress, and plan how to move forward.
- Run monthly reports (Ranking Report, AdWords, Analytics, etc.).
- Put together key feedback for a meeting or recap message.
- Do live meetings via Join, Zoom, or other video conferencing tools where clients and others can see your screen.
- Send a follow-up email with key items covered.
- If a meeting can't be arranged, then an email recap should be sent each month.
- Develop a quarterly strategy for each client.
- Update chart of accounts along with status.
- Send a recap email in the absence of a meeting.
- Respond to client emails proactively (within the same business day).
- Answer client's inbound calls & deal with requests as needed.
- Document tickets & follow through on open items for clients.
- Follow up on tickets weekly to ensure they are in progress & close the loop with clients.

Compensation

You will want to pay your account manager between $45K - $85K salary. You could offer compensation on a sliding scale as they get trained up & add value:

- This is a $55K per year position + bonuses.
- During the training period of 90 days, you will earn $45K.
- Once you get out of that first 90 days and start to take on your first accounts, your payment will be increased to $55K.
- Once you have a full load of accounts and are fully trained (30-35 clients), your payment will be increased to $85K.

You could also incentivize the account manager based on client retention & up-sells.

- 20% of the first-month billing increase (depending upon service up-sold).
- $500 quarterly bonus as long as retention is greater than 97%.

You can use these lists to start your own job description, customizing them to the needs of your agency. Remember to be detailed so you can attract the right candidate who has experience doing what you are requesting.

Besides responsibilities and requirements, it is also important to include in a job description the targets and benchmarks you would expect from your account manager. This gives them the details of what they'd expect to accomplish on a daily, weekly, and monthly basis.

Targets & Benchmarks You Should Expect:

- Retaining current agency accounts every month.
- Making upsells.
- Collecting client reviews.
- Holding regular review meetings with clients.
- Acting as a liaison between the client and your agency—conveying information and ensuring a smooth lead-flow process while managing client accounts.
- Making the client aware of other services and actions that may lead to greater success—Upsells.
- Monitoring the client's budget, explaining costs, and negotiating new terms if necessary.
- Keeping up on trends, changes, and competitor actions that might affect the client, i.e., social media policy changes, advertising rules, etc.
- Negotiating contracts and closing agreements to maximize profits.
- Providing progress reports to clients and upper management.
- Acting as an initiator and nurturing your lead flow.
- Growing current accounts.

With these details, you'll be able to put together a stellar job description that will generate your ideal candidate list in no time.

Interview For An Account Manager

Once you place your job posts, you will get all sorts of responses. You'll want a process you can use to weed out the candidates to narrow down your list to a handful. One of the ways you can do this from the beginning is to set up a pre-screening process.

This process works for most agencies:

- Have them send a video/voicemail intro to ensure they have strong English-speaking skills & that the accent won't be an issue. We use VideoAsk for this.

- Ask them to describe their experience with the requirements you have posted in the job description.

- Have them answer, "Why do you want to work for my agency?" and similar questions.

- Have them take a Kolbe or DISC Assessment (RepStack offers one free Kolbe Assessment if you choose to work with us).

By doing a pre-screening process, you can find your perfect account manager a lot faster. You'll be surprised how many applicants don't want to do the pre-screening test because they consider it too hard. Those that are eager to do the pre-employment screening are the dedicated ones who are eager to work for you—they show their dedication from the very beginning.

Phase 1 — Submitting a video resume

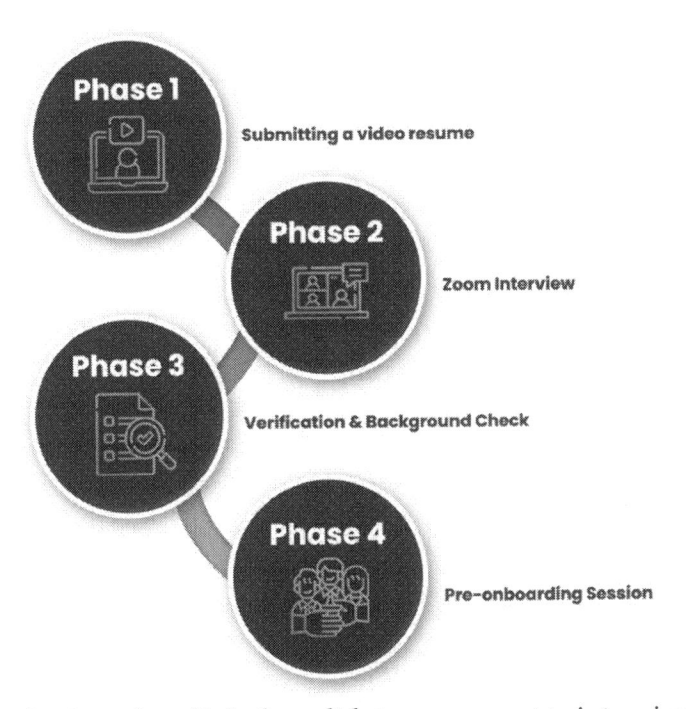

Phase 2 — Zoom Interview

Phase 3 — Verification & Background Check

Phase 4 — Pre-onboarding Session

After selecting a handful of candidates, you want to interview, it's time to start preparing your interview questions. The questions should be based on the information you included in your job description. In general, you'll want to ask, during the interview, about their previous experience completing tasks that match the requirements and responsibilities in your job post. It's reassuring to hear a candidate describe, in detail, similar tasks they've done previously.

You can also ask them questions such as:

- Why did you leave your previous digital marketing agency?
- What are your strengths, and what do you feel you do best?

- What interested you in this position?

- Are you able to commit full-time to this position and be dedicated to working just for my agency?

- Can you give an example of when you were on the phone with an upset client and what you did to resolve the issue?

Tailor your questions around the situations your account manager is most likely to encounter. Think about your current situation as your agency's account manager and the difficult moments you have with your current clients. Ask your candidates similar questions to see how they will react in the same situation.

One thing that is beneficial to do during an interview is a roleplaying scenario. Since an account manager needs to have exceptional customer service skills and be able to create personal relationships with clients, have them work through a tough situation as you act as a client. Then you'll be able to see how they react and what process they would go through to find a solution.

By following the process above, you'll be able to narrow down your list of candidates and find the perfect one to join your team. Once you've found your new account manager, it's time to start onboarding them so they can start using their talents and skills right away.

Onboarding Your New Account Manager

For all of my remote associates, I provide a 90-day onboarding training program that is tailored to the tasks I expect them to complete. I have a unique program for all three key roles that the associate will complete in a timely manner while tackling their daily tasks.

90 Day RepStack Success Academy Training Plan

	Month 1 (Day 1-30)	Month 2 (Day 30-60)	Month 3 (Day 60-90)
Week 1	o Fundamentals of Digital Marketing o HighLevel and CRM Masterclass o Email Deliverability & Email Builders	o Social Media Marketing Certification o Google Analytics, GA4 o Google Tag Manager	o SEO Training Certifications o SEO Advance Level Training o On Page and Off Page SEO
Week 2	o Cold Outreach o Cold Email Marketing o MailChimp o Active Campaign	o Facebook Business Manager o Facebook Ads Manager o Social Media Marketing Mastery	o Data and Extensive Keyword Research o SEMrush, Ahrefs o WordPress Website Development
Week 3	o Automations and Triggers o Dream 100	o Facebook Meta Certifications	o WordPress Training

	o Hillsberg Method o Chat Bot Integration o CRM Workflows	o Google Search Ads o Google Display Network o Google Ads Training	o Facebook Ad Creatives o Dollar A Day o Content Syndication
Week 4	o Basic Keyword Research o Content Marketing o Marketing Copy	o GMB Certification o LinkedIn Ads o TikTok Ads Mastery o YouTube Ads	o Content Marketing o Podcasts and Webinars o Video Editing and Graphic Design

All sorts of training courses are available online through popular platforms such as Udemy.com. They offer your account managers certifications and provide them with the needed education to excel in your agency. In addition to onboarding training, you'll also want to create a checklist for your account manager to complete so that they can become familiar with your agency, your software, and all of their new responsibilities.

An example checklist can be:

- Introduction to the agency's culture and work ethic.
- Baseline training and assessment for your CRM.
- Setup of all tools and software before day 1.

- Initiate communication and daily reports to gauge communication style.
- Stress-test work-from-home setup:
    - Internet speed: minimum 15mbs
    - Power backup in place
    - Work laptop with the right hardware provided to the associate
    - Any additional hardware needed to do the job provided
    - VPN
    - Home Office Setup verified
    - Setup of Time Doctor to track time and tasks
    - Camera and lighting

In addition to the account manager's checklist of tasks to complete during their first week with your agency, here are some other things to consider before they start work:

- What tools need to be set up for them? Who will set those up? Create a checklist.
- What will their orientation process look like?
    - Initial Day
    - Accessing Tools / Software
- How will they be trained in what you expect them to do?
    - Orientation on the roll

- Training on the day-to-day
- What will they be expected to report daily/weekly/monthly?
- How will you gauge their performance?
- Communicate the expectations!

As you prepare your account manager to get started, ensure that you have a process in place that will help them be onboarded into their new position in a timely manner. You'll be able to avoid so many problems by putting this process into place from the very beginning and allowing your account manager to be self-sufficient. One agency owner I spoke with admitted that after several bottlenecks, in the beginning, he eventually dropped the ball and hired an account manager. He never regretted his decisions, as the results were amazing.

Ongoing Training, Management, & Accountability

Once your new account manager gets settled into their new role, you'll want to have ongoing training for your associate to ensure their continued success and commitment to the agency. In addition, you'll want a process that will enable you to manage your account manager and keep them in a routine of accountability. Decide when they will meet with you for a feedback session and how you will continue to train and develop them.

Below are RepStack-only processes, but you should have something similar present if you hire outside of RepStack:

- → Continuous training inside our Training Academy | RepStack Success Academy
- → Custom training courses from World Class Business Coaches such as:
    - ◆ Josh Nelson | Seven Figure Agency
    - ◆ Andrew Cass | PipelinePRO
    - ◆ Alex Schlinsky | Prospecting on Demand
    - ◆ Dennis Yu | BlitzMetrics
- → Weekly Associate Check-ins
- → Monthly Client Check-ins
- → Time Tracking Application: RepStack uses Time Doctor, while Upwork uses its native software.
- → Tracking EOD reports

By putting a process into place that tracks the tasks of your account managers, you'll then be able to see what sort of training they might need. To upscale your account manager, keep them updated on all the latest training.

Accountability is an important part of managing all your associates. Below is an example of the end-of-the-day report I received from my account managers so I can see which tasks they could complete in one day.

Account Manager End-Of-Day Reports Example:

Today's workflow:

- Checking review email for GM2 - Blogs
- Checked on all SEO reports
- Checked on all the GMB calendar posts for:
  1. Ace Tree
  2. Clark Tree Experts
  3. Coastal Tree Trimmers
  4. Island Tree Service
  5. Southern Tree Pros
  6. Stevens Tree Services
  7. Tree Workers of Phoenix
  8. Trees N Scapes Unlimited
  9. Tri-State Tree Services
  10. Urban Jacks Tree Service
  11. Volunteer Tree Company
- Created Website Cosmo sheet for Country Trees
- Created PPC and Landing page sheets for Country Trees LLC
- Created a new tracking / CallRail number for Southern Trees
- Marked off GMB task for Arborist Aboard
- Marked off AA review task for Bumblebee

- Checking emails sent to Bumblebee - Blogs

Nothing is more reassuring than to receive a detailed end-of-day report from my account manager. Not only will you be able to see how an account manager can take over the tasks you are used to doing with your clients, but they will more than likely exceed your expectations.

In the next chapter, you'll be able to read real-life case studies of successful agency owners and their experiences and growth when they brought on an account manager. These stories are from agency owners who went through the same process to first hire a marketing associate, then a sales development representative, and finally an account manager to close the loop.

Chapter 12:

The Account Manager Case Studies

An account manager is one of the secret weapons to building a successful digital marketing agency. Many digital marketing agencies have started realizing this and are fast recruiting them onboard.

The role of the account manager is vital to your digital marketing agency. They make client retention possible. As much as acquiring new clients is every agency's dream, retention is crucial. Retention is the ability to maintain former clients by creating a long-term beneficial relationship and partnership with them. This makes them well-satisfied and committed to your agency.

As you may have already known, the goal of any agency is to achieve these two things: (1) close deals to take on new clients and (2) retain your current list of clients. That's the only way for any business to grow. If you take on new clients and you lose your former clients, that is stagnancy and therefore signifies zero growth and development in your agency. If you focus your strategies on client retention and hire an account manager that is equal to the task, you can put your mind at ease and make six figures in no time.

This chapter shifts away from the theoretical aspect discussed in the previous chapter and focuses on actual results and testimonies from well-satisfied top clients. Here, you get to see firsthand real-life cases that show the importance of having an account manager in your agency.

The case studies in this chapter dwell on how account managers work for their agencies to retain the list of current clients and offer amazing customer service. What is powerful about these case studies is that they give you realistic expectations of what to expect from your account manager. You'll be able to see the varying tasks they complete and how they go about it, giving you a clear idea of how an account manager can benefit your agency.

The most notable characteristic of these account managers is the short space of time it took them to settle in with their agency and start making progress. Some of them have already gotten promoted to senior positions within their first year. This shows these account managers have been able to provide so much for their agency owners. By applying the onboarding process described in the previous chapter, you can expect to experience similar results as in the case studies below.

Let's begin with Wesley Smith, the CEO of Tree Service Digital.

How the CEO of Tree Service Digital had an Incredible Experience Working with an Account Manager

REPSTACK CASE STUDY

SHE HAS JUMPED IN AND LEARNT OUR SYSTEM, OUR PROCESSES AND HOW TO MANAGE OUR ACCOUNTS

WESLEY SMITH | ALIZAY HAMDANI

I must admit the testimonial from Wesley Smith, CEO of Tree Service Digital, was one of the best I have ever received. He couldn't hide his excitement and proudly told us how profitable his business has been since hiring an account manager from RepStack. We at RepStack work with agencies like Tree Service Digital with a laid down workable system and an achievable purpose that will allow their team members to thrive and showcase their potential to the maximum. What I found special when speaking with Wesley is how customer-oriented he is. Since leaving his former employer, who he worked with for so many years, and starting his own agency, he has stuck to one niche (Tree Services) and devised methods to solve his clients' problems and help them grow their businesses. I could see how alike we were in our passion for achieving customer satisfaction. The only difference is I focus on helping numerous digital marketing agencies grow, not just Tree Service agencies.

For an agency like Tree Service Digital that puts so much time, effort, and resources into helping its clients, it is essential to employ the right workforce who is client-oriented and goal-driven—someone that will keep their agency running smoothly and prevent it from going bankrupt. But, instead, make it blossom financially. If there's any team member directly linked to achieving this, it is the account manager. Wesley recognized this fact and considered hiring an account manager who would help him manage his day-to-day tasks. It is popularly said birds of a feather flock together. On speaking with Wesley Smith, the CEO of Tree Service Digital, he saw how passionate I was about what I do and how greatly we could help him smoothly reach his dream of optimally serving tree contractors. He decided to have onboard one of our account managers. Now he can proudly say that was one of the best decisions he has made for his agency. In the short time he hired one of our account managers, his agency has experienced a massive boost and noticeable growth in sales.

We spoke at length, and he described his experience working with his RepStack account manager as a delightful experience. Here is what he had to say:

"We hired a RepStack account manager roughly two to three months ago and she has been incredible. Her name is Alizay and she has jumped in and learnt our system, our processes and how to manage our accounts, and so far, so good I see big things for her moving on—and we are going to come back to you guys pretty soon for a second one."

As much as I know my account managers always deliver, I greatly enjoyed hearing it from a top client like Tree Service Digital. From his testimony, it is crystal clear he is immensely satisfied with the services of his RepStack account manager, Alizay. She has retained top clients for his agency and has significantly increased the company's profits. No wonder he wants to hire a second account manager!

Also, there is this question I sometimes get from people that an account manager ought to be US based. I decided to ask Wesley if that has been an issue for him with Alizay, and here's what he said:

"To be honest, I had a similar concern before I started. But I have come to realize that what matters is she has great English speaking, writing, and email marketing skills, among other things. To answer your question, the fact that she isn't US-based has not been an issue."

"She works very hard. In fact, harder than the instate folks."

All Alizay is doing is working and bringing great returns and sales for her client's agency. Come with me, and let's take a peek into her daily scheduled tasks as a RepStack accountant manager at Tree Service Digital Company. See firsthand what exactly she does that makes her client see her as an indispensable partner – crucial to their agency's success.

"I am an account manager with Tree Service Digital. I just want to show you how my day typically goes. The first thing I do is log into my Time Doctor so that my time in is marked. Then I go ahead and check my emails. I reply back to each customer if there's a query. Since I usually receive their quotes from their landing pages, I can easily determine how many clients are getting their leads and their calls. I have thirty clients in total."

"Moving forward, I go into Teamwork, check each and every one of my clients and check which tasks need to be done on that day or that week."

"I have a sheet containing all the clients and their details; I go through the details of each client and see what needs to be done. For example, if they have an update or something new that just came up that needs to be done. After that, I go ahead and check the GMB post for each client and update them."

"I check the Google My Business posts to see what needs to be done on a weekly basis but since I have a large number of clients, it needs to be checked every other day, just so I don't miss out on anyone. Then I go ahead and check the Google ads to see if everything is running smoothly."

"I also check the agency's outlet if the SEO report is all done and smooth. I check the spider reports and the calls if everything is running smoothly. If some clients need any assistance, I go ahead and update my manager about it. I also ask if it is something I can do so I can be of help. I make sure to update that in the sheet. I mostly check my emails because they keep coming in every now and then. I also check the press releases, which is done monthly for every client. That is about all."

Aliza's keen eye for detail, enthusiasm for work, and thoroughness, among other things, can be seen in all her statements. And they play a key role in how she has brought about the growth and development of her client's digital marketing agency.

Our account managers have the right skill set to manage and grow your most valued accounts to maximize mutual value and achieve mutually beneficial goals. They can further help by looking at how they can add value to your clients. From operations to sales or marketing, our account manager explores ways to improve various aspects of your client's business. That way, they perform the major role they are known for- client retention.

How the Owner of TopLine Growth made Tremendous Progress Working with an Account Manager

REPSTACK CASE STUDY

IT WAS SUPER EASY TO GET STARTED. THE WHOLE PROCESS WAS REALLY QUICK AND SEAMLESS.

FORREST SCHWARTZ | SIKANDER SHEHZAD

"You can't be a jack of all trades, and expect your agency to grow." That's one of the first things Forrest Schwartz said when he spoke with our client success manager. Forrest Schwartz is the CEO of TopLine Growth. Two decades ago, he learned to crack the business development code, left the agency he was working with, and built his own marketing agency.

Forrest Schwartz observed that most digital marketing agencies are 'jack of all trades' in that they don't have the right professionals in place to execute tasks that will give the agency tangible results.

Many agency owners try to do all the tasks on their own or hire an in-house employee only to get less-than-ideal outcomes at the end of the day. When he said, "You can't be a jack of all trades", that resonated with me, and I couldn't agree more. You cannot do it all on your own that is why you need the skillset of proven professionals to grow your agency. Forrest Schwartz recognized this and hired a RepStack account manager who would bring him tangible results, transparent reports, and a remarkable profit rise. Now he has Sikander Shehzad, a RepStack account manager that solves his problems constantly, manages his internal and external communications, and drives his projects to completion.

Forrest Schwartz spoke with us and told us about his delightful experience since hiring Sikander in his workforce.

"I have been working with RepStack for about three months, specifically with Sikander. He is my account manager and the experience so far has been really great. It was super easy to get started."

"The process was really well thought out. They went through what I was looking for, what I needed and recommended some candidates. We hit it off right away. After the process, he was onboard, in about two weeks or so. It was really quick and seamless."

"I'm really enjoying it. I have been making progress since three months and I couldn't be happier. I just want to tell everyone that you are bound to have the same experience."

It always gladdens my heart to hear positive news like this from my clients. It shows the work my team and I put into helping digital marketing agencies hasn't been futile. In addition, the skill, knowledge, and expertise we have put together over the years have been proven strong, reliable, and viable enough to bring about amazing results and a high financial turnover when applied to the letter.

Let's go on a quick trip through the daily activities of TopLine Growth's account manager– Sikander Shehzad. See why he is a great fit for TopLine Growth and exactly what they need.

"I am RepStack's digital account manager and marketing executive, currently working with TopLine Growth. I'm going to take a couple of minutes to show you what my daily activities look like. Firstly, I make sure I'm logged into Time Doctor, which tracks my time throughout the day."

"Then I go over to Slack to see if there are any new updates or messages from any of my clients; or any tasks that may require my assistance or response. For tasks and product management, I use ClickUp. On it, I can see all the tasks that I have been assigned and which I can work on. Also with it, I can manage my team along with the tasks I have assigned them. It shows all the time estimation, the due dates, and the urgency that my client requires for a particular task."

"Secondly, we use GoHighLevel, one of the most important tools of our agency. We have all our clients on this particular tool. From automations and web flows to pipelines and landing pages, each and everything is on this tool because it is very crucial for the work we do."

"That is not all, I am also working on the marketing side of my client which requires Facebook setups, ad campaign setups, and podcasts mainly. Currently, I'm scheduling and uploading all the podcasts and also, other podcasts directories like Spotify, SoundCloud and apple podcasts. I have also been working on the Google ad campaigns of all my clients that are assigned to me, to see if they are actually running well and they are generating public pixels, running GMB posts and pulling all the viewers and creatives."

"I'm responsible for all the Facebook ad campaigns. I set up campaigns, write ad copies. I pull out creatives and review if they are performing well and if they require any changes. That is a quick rundown of how my day with TopLine Growth actually seems like."

After hearing what Sikander had to say, I must admit that he had quite a busy day there. His day is so packed, yet well organized and detailed. It is amazing and highly commendable how effectively he juggles the role of an account manager and a marketing executive. It is practically impossible not to see amazing results in TopLine Growth and an ecstatic CEO when you have a dedicated multitasker like Sikander Shehzad on your team.

The Owner of Raxxar Digital Marketing Agency Shared Positive Testimony for Having an Account Manager as a Part of His Team

REPSTACK CASE STUDY

ACCOUNT MANAGER CASE STUDY: ASMAA

LYN ASKIN | ASMAA KHAN

After having some conversations with Lyn Askin, the owner of Raxxar Digital Marketing Agency, I found something unique about him—he is an industry expert and is very good at what he does. After working with several digital marketing agencies, Lyn Askin decided to found his own agency. He founded Raxxar Digital Marketing Agency about 15 years ago in Lafayette, LA, to meet his clients' marketing and SEO needs.

Lyn is an expert at finding solutions for small business owners, especially regarding website design, marketing, and SEO. But where he excelled in his niche, he had difficulties retaining his old clients and keeping up with his new ones.

That's when he decided to bring Asmaa Khan onto his team—an account manager who was a professional in his agency's niche. With Asmaa on his team, he hit all his new account management targets for his agency.

Lyn has experienced nothing but excellence while working with Asmaa. His agency's main goal is to help its clients increase their revenue through digital marketing, and Asmaa helped him achieve that. When he brought on his new account manager, I was interested to hear directly from him about his thought on having this new associate on his team. Just like I knew, Asmaa's dedication, passion, and love for her work didn't escape the attention of Lyn Askin. Here is what he has to say about Asmaa Khan.

"I am Lyn from Raxxar Digital Marketing and I just have to give a positive testimony for RepStack. RepStack connected us with Asmaa, to be a part of our team. She has been amazing so far and she has done everything we have asked her to. She is very proactive and eager to learn. We are excited to have her as a part of our team. And I'm really looking forward to growing with her and RepStack. Thank you, RepStack. We really appreciate this."

This testimony is an example of great customer service delivered by our RepStack account manager. Since Asmaa joined his team, Lyn has seen incredible growth in the company. He is delighted to have Asmaa as part of his team because she is eager to learn, acts in advance, and always ensures her work is well prioritized.

Just a few months after Lyn and Asmaa started working together, our client success manager touched base with Asmaa to hear how she was doing. Not only was she enjoying working with Raxxar, but she was also getting to use all her strengths and potential to generate incredible results for the agency.

Here is a little tour into the day of Asmaa Khan, a RepStack account manager at Raxxar Digital Marketing Agency:

"Today I will be giving you a peek into my day as a virtual account manager, so let's get started. First of all, I open my Time Doctor and make sure it is running well. After which I update my signing in through Slack. I move forward to the Help Scout in boxes and check all the emails from my clients. If there are any urgent emails, I respond to them and add notes to them as well."

"If there are any updates from my clients or tasks that need to be done, I communicate them to my team. I create different tasks for different team members depending on the type of task they are required to do based on their job description. Apart from assigning tasks to my team members on Teamwork, I check the tasks assigned to me and complete them."

"Also, I create projects on Teamwork and whatever new projects or new clients we have, I add them on Teamwork. I update project briefs and communicate with my clients on any requirements we need before we can start working on their project. Apart from that, I review all the submitted contents from my team and once that is done, I give a heads up to the team members to complete the task on Teamwork. I move toward the next step, which entails checking if the content and design have been completed. If that has been done, I assign the next task to our web developer: code the design. Once that has been done, we get it approved by the client." Apart from communicating with the clients and team members, I manage the monthly press releases for our SEO clients. They are about twenty in number. There are some press releases I have recently published. Once I have published the press releases or passed them, I hand them over to my team members. I update all the information in the spreadsheet, there I indicate if it has been written or published. We have a project pulse document where we write all what the client needs and we update it every time the need arises. For example, when I start a project, I put down everything in the Project Pulse document—starting from how far we have gone with the design and content and if we are done with it, and if so, if the design has been sent to where it gets coded. Apart from that, if there are any queries from our clients or my team members, I write them there as well. This is to make sure these queries are addressed on time."

"In addition, I take my GoHighLevel training on ClickUp on a daily basis. If there is any urgent task that needs to be completed, I do that as well. I recently updated the SMTP2GO plugin on about ten websites that were not working properly. Also, I curated headings and description for two of our clients for their PPC ad campaigns."

"At the end of the day, I always create a proper end report for my employer, Lyn Askin, and send them over to him through Slack. That's about it. Thank you."

Asmaa Khan is a team player who professionally oversees her team members and communicates anything needed to them while still performing her tasks to perfection. It brings me great joy to see her putting all that energy into being a great account manager and team leader who delegates duties efficiently and seamlessly for the smooth running of her client's operations. Her commitment to timely documentation did not escape her agency's notice. You will be surprised by how much chaos and problems failure to document important details could cause for your client's agency. The last thing you want is for your client to take their business elsewhere. Asmaa also creates a detailed end-of-day report, which she sends to her employer: This keeps him in the loop of things, and if there's any issue at all, that way he can easily see it, point it out and address it early before it poses a bigger problem in the future.

Whereas in previous chapters, we have discussed the importance of other job roles, the fact that I discussed the role of an account manager last doesn't make it any less important than all the others. And these testimonies corroborate my point that the role of an account manager is just as key to making clients happy and willing to stick with your digital marketing agency alone. We all know a satisfied client signifies a successful and advancing agency.

From the case studies we have just looked at together, you can see how all the account managers have devoted their knowledge, experience, and skills to satisfy every need of their clients. They have provided optimum client satisfaction and retention and have massively boosted their clients' finances—all in just a few months of working with their respective agencies. At RepStack, you not only get what you want, but you also get what you had no idea you needed. We are all about making our clients happy and skyrocketing their finances while at it. Our clients' experience about sums it all up. And just like the CEO of TopLine Growth, Forrest Schwartz, said: "You are likely to have the same experience."

Conclusion

I wish I could tell you that hiring for just one or two of the job roles mentioned in this book will give your digital marketing agency a financial turnover. But the truth is, it won't. It would be best if you had the combined effort of all three underdogs to see a tangible result and achieve the tremendous outcome you desire.

This book is a practical guide that reveals how you can reach that $1 million mark for your digital marketing agency. The easy-to-follow process provided in the book shows exactly how to reach that number in the next twenty-four to thirty-six months. All you have to do is follow it to the letter.

The book also provides real-life examples of agency owners who were once stuck in a vicious circle, doing marketing, sales, and account management for their agency, but later realized that they could move away from the busy day-to-day work and let their business run on its own.

So many agencies are still stuck in their traditional ways instead of grabbing the opportunity social media offers and monetizing it greatly. My years as a struggling CEO weren't easy or yielding as many returns as I wanted until I realized I couldn't take on every job role, no matter how good I thought I was. I will be honest, the first major step I took towards attaining my financial freedom was hiring a business coach. In chapter one, I explained in detail who a STUCK agency owner was and how to identify one.

With the help of my coach, I discovered the three key roles for agency growth, which include:

- A marketing associate

- A sales development representative
- An account manager

Delegating my tasks to these three associates and trusting them with responsibilities was the beginning of my success story.

A success story I decided to pen down in this book to help other digital marketing agencies like mine. I fully understand the struggles you are experiencing with your marketing agency. It might be hard to believe, but at some point, in my life, I also struggled to be financially stable in my business. I took on the role of every worker an agency needed. Although I was great at assigning work for content creation, social media, SEO, and web development, I struggled to be the marketing associate, sales development rep, and account manager – the key roles a good agency should never take with levity. I did not know of this back then, and I kept doing everything in my business myself. It wasn't long before I got burned out from being pulled in too many directions. Meanwhile, my agency was still stagnant, and the real breakthrough didn't come despite all I had put myself through to change my story for the better. It was not until I learned not to do everything myself but to delegate my tasks to the three key members discussed so far in this book that I began to record the desired success.

Before I started my own digital marketing agency, I was a salesman working for Best Buy. I did that for seven years as I developed my personal techniques for bringing in big sales. It was my hero's journey as I slowly moved away from the life I had been living as an introvert and learned how to connect with people. I connected with people from around the world and provided them with marketing solutions that skyrocketed their businesses. It was then that I got the motivation to start my own digital marketing agency. However, my agency struggled to have the same type of progress because I was so focused on fulfilling the needs of others that I relegated my own needs to the background. I merely reaped what I had sown. That went on for some time until I finally took the plunge and made deliberate efforts by sacrificing my time, effort, and resources for the feasible goal I had in mind – The goal of reaching the 1 million dollars mark. After 13 grueling years, I finally achieved it!

My current goal is to help other digital marketing agencies achieve the same but in a shorter time. Now you are at the end of the book. You are fully equipped with all the techniques I developed over the years. I emphasized hiring the right associates to grow your business in the book. It is of utmost importance to employ them at the right time and in the right order. There is a process: hiring, onboarding, and training. You have to train and coach them if you must achieve success. Please do not overlook this step because it contributes to how well they connect with you and integrate into your company's purpose and vision, which is vital to helping you achieve your goal.

To hire them correctly, you have to start with the Marketing Associate. Below are their major duties:

- Managing cold outreach campaigns:
- Taking care of your social media profiles and posting regular updates.
- Overseeing time launch and managing paid ad campaigns.
- Managing the CRM system to assist the sales and marketing teams.

- Building funnels and putting them in place.

Major Benefits of Hiring a Marketing Associate:

- They free up your time: you can now take a step back from the day-to-day task of creating marketing campaigns.
- They lower your overhead costs.
- They scale your agency's operations and increase all the other mechanics of your agency.
- They strengthen the weak part of your agency by providing a pipeline of extra skill sets.
- They are always available 24/7 and can step in for you when the need arises.

To get the right marketing associate, you must look out for the following when hiring them:

- Enthusiasm about digital marketing
- Clear communication skills to easily work with all other team members
- Already holds in-depth knowledge of digital marketing techniques
- Excellent interpersonal skills
- Ability to work with strict deadlines
- After this, you are one job role ahead of your financial worries

The next job role is the Sales Development Representative (SDR), and these are their roles in your agency:

- Cleaning up" your prospect list
- Answering and directing 70-80 phone calls a day
- Managing communication and answering emails
- Preparing and organizing databases and reports
- Managing social media accounts and replies
- Handling customer and employer information confidentially
- Taking notes and transcribing meetings conducted online and sharing minutes of the meetings.
- Scheduling meetings and managing your calendar and appointments
- Creating purchase orders, tracking and managing payments
- Managing filing systems, updating records, and organizing documentation
- Researching online for materials and sources for presentations
- Ensuring all calls are started via your CRMs (HighLevel, HubSpot, etc.) as recommended, so there is an accurate log of activity & calls are recorded.
- Ensuring each call/message has an outcome noted in your CRM.
- Setting scheduled appointments using your calendar link (your sales assistant can set that up for you).

With time, you will be able to rely on your sales development representative to make discovery calls and book strategy sessions to close deals on their own.

These are the major benefits of hiring a Sales Development Representative:

- Saving your time and money
- Expanding your sales force
- Providing cost-effective solutions
- Going over and beyond for your agency as they are a new breed of sales developers
- Generating and nurturing leads
- Gathering valuable data and analyzing them
- Dedicating their skill set to your agency
- Helping you to take care of the tasks you dislike

These are the right requirements to look for when hiring a Sales Development Representative:

- Superior written and verbal communication skills
- A bachelor's degree or relevant experience
- Business Management experience would be preferred
- Outgoing and candid personality
- Ability to work under pressure and meet deadlines
- A proactive, solution-oriented, and out-of-the-box thinker

- Ability to learn new tools

The last job role is the account manager. Below is the wide range of duties they perform:

- Meeting with clients at least once per month to review reports and progress and make plans on how to move forward
- Running monthly reports (Ranking Report, AdWords, Analytics).
- Putting together critical feedback for a meeting or recap message.
- Doing live meetings via Join, Zoom, or some other video conferencing tools
- Sending a follow-up email with key items covered.
- Developing a quarterly strategy for each client.
- Updating chart of accounts along with status.
- Sending a recap email in the absence of a meeting.
- Responding to client emails proactively (within the same business day).
- Answering inbound client calls & dealing with requests as needed.
- Documenting tickets & follow-through on open items for clients.
- Doing a Follow-up on tickets weekly to ensure they are in progress & closing the loop with clients.

Here is the list of responsibilities and requirements I use when looking to hire an account manager:

- Proven work experience as an account manager
- Demonstratable ability to communicate, present and influence key stakeholders at all levels of an organization
- Solid experience with CRM software (GoHighLevel, Zoho CRM, or HubSpot) and MS Office (particularly MS Excel)
- Experience delivering client-focused solutions to customer needs
- Proven ability to juggle multiple account management projects at a time while maintaining sharp attention to detail
- Excellent listening, negotiation, and presentation abilities
- Strong verbal and written communication skills
- BA/BS degree in Business Administration, Sales, or a relevant field

Major Benefits of Hiring an Account Manager:

- Developing long-term relationships with a portfolio of clients.
- Connecting with key business executives and stakeholders to maintain long-term relationships and gain continued renewal of services.
- Retaining current agency accounts every month.

- Keeping up on trends, changes, and competitor actions that might affect the clients, i.e., social media policy changes, advertising rules, etc.
- Making upsells.
- Collecting client reviews.
- Holding regular review meetings with clients.
- Acting as a liaison between the client and your agency - conveying information, and ensuring a smooth lead-flow process, while managing client accounts.
- Making the client aware of other services and actions that may lead to greater success.
- Monitoring the client's budget, explaining costs, and negotiating new terms if necessary.
- Negotiating contracts and closing agreements to maximize profits
- Providing progress reports to clients and upper management
- Growing current accounts

These three job roles are the backbone and pillars of any digital marketing agency. One good thing about having these key members in your team is that they are usually dedicated and available to work with you long-term; plus, you can find these highly-skilled individuals anywhere in the world. Meanwhile, if your agency is not earning up to $10,000 per month, you can decide to hire one or two of these roles; preferably, start with a marketing associate.

As I mentioned earlier, I shared some testimonies and real-life cases from our top clients in this book. They gave authenticity to all the three pillars of a fully automated digital marketing agency I discussed in this book. They also showed you that your dream of making 1 million dollars in the next 2 to 3 years is feasible and attainable. You have only one task; religiously follow the strategy written in this book.

Are you ready to take the net worth of your digital marketing agency to six figures?

Bonus Chapter!

The Executive Assistant Advantage

An Executive Assistant is a professional who is responsible for managing and planning key business initiatives while acting as a bridge across various departments as well as being the point of contact for external partners.

As the right hand to a business executive, your executive assistant will be the forerunner in providing you with guidance and strategic counsel to expedite key decisions. With ensured stellar support for execution of operations their expertise makes them a key player for any team.

I recommend hiring this role after you have filled all the other 3 roles inside your agency.

Why should you hire an Executive Assistant?

Are you feeling overwhelmed by the chaos of organization and communication? Let me introduce you to an Executive Assistants. Having one at your side is like discovering a new superpower – all of your struggles with inbox/email management, scheduling appointments on your calendar, managing your social media and other organizational tasks will suddenly become effortless.

Not only that, but understand that their entire focus is trained on you gaining success in your agency: they concentrate on providing order and structure to keep your workday running smoothly without fail. Efficiency and effectiveness are what makes an Executive Assistant so valuable to have!

Responsibilities of an Executive Assistant

If you're still wondering why, you need an Executive Assistant, here are the top 5 reasons you should hire for this key role.

1. **You have an overflowing inbox that you need to manage.** Delegate email management to your Executive Assistants who are pros at being organized and thorough.

2. **You want to be active on social media but you don't have time.** It's important to have a social media presence in this day and age, your EA is the key to personal branding and networking.

3. **You want someone to manage your calendars and schedule meetings.** Let your Executive Assistant help you navigate through meetings each day through excellent coordination and correspondence.

4. **You want someone to manage projects and supervise clerical personnel.** Make your event and project management a breeze - turn it over to your Executive Assistant. With their help, you don't have to worry about the nitty-gritty of planning and execution.

5. **You want to spend more time with family while not thinking about business.** Unlock your business' potential for growth by entrusting repetitive tasks to an Executive Assistant - freeing up valuable time and energy for you.

SALVA MALIK | EXECUTIVE ASSISTANT

Some of their tasks include:

- Handling administrative tasks
- Organizing and managing your work day
- Maintaining an executive presence
- Planning and managing events

Looking over all of the tasks they will cover, you will find that having an extra set of hands-on deck creates a seamless workflow - making sure projects are running smoothly while creating lasting impressions with prospects & partners alike!

Not only do they bring professionalism and team-building initiatives but their proficiency in Calendar Management, social media & CRMs ensure professionalism like never before - so what more could you want? With just one hire, you're guaranteed elevated results across many levels instantly.

Your Executive Assistant does not only provide administrative support, but also manage social media presence with finesse. Once familiarized with your style of communication and brand identity, these experts curate a similar tone that resonates with your niche. Yet still impress them with expertise and professionalism

It doesn't stop there - besides business communications their creativity allows them run team-building activities efficiently so that projects can effectively take flight!

Your Executive Assistant is the perfect guide to bring your targets within reach. For example, if you've got multiple goals this quarter, they will help map out and streamline each step until it's done!

Here are some benefits of hiring an Executive Assistant:

1. **Time management:** An executive assistant can help you manage your time more effectively by taking care of tasks such as scheduling, email management, and travel arrangements. This frees up your time to focus on the most important tasks and goals.

2. **Increased productivity:** With an executive assistant handling the administrative work, you'll have more time to focus on the tasks that require your expertise and attention. This can lead to increased productivity and better results for your company.

3. **Improved organization:** An executive assistant can help you stay organized by keeping track of important documents, deadlines, and meetings. This can help reduce stress and ensure that you're always prepared.

4. **Enhanced communication:** An executive assistant can act as a gatekeeper and filter out unnecessary or unimportant communications, allowing you to focus on the most

important messages. They can also help you keep track of important contacts and follow up on important tasks.

5. **Increased professionalism:** An executive assistant can help improve the overall professionalism of your business by handling tasks such as managing your calendar, scheduling appointments, and handling incoming calls in a professional manner.

Overall, an executive assistant can help you be more efficient, organized, and productive, allowing you to focus on the tasks that are most important to your business.

Made in the USA
Columbia, SC
01 October 2023